The Butterfly Book

If my first glance of the morning was for the sun, my first thought was for the butterflies it would engender.
— VLADIMIR NABOKOV, *Speak, Memory*

STOKES NATURE GUIDES

BY DONALD STOKES

A Guide to Nature in Winter
A Guide to Observing Insect Lives
A Guide to Bird Behavior, Volume I

BY DONALD AND LILLIAN STOKES

A Guide to Bird Behavior, Volume II
A Guide to Bird Behavior, Volume III
A Guide to Enjoying Wildflowers
A Guide to Animal Tracking and Behavior

BY THOMAS F. TYNING

A Guide to Amphibians and Reptiles

STOKES BACKYARD NATURE BOOKS

BY DONALD AND LILLIAN STOKES

The Bird Feeder Book
The Hummingbird Book
The Complete Birdhouse Book
The Bluebird Book

ALSO BY DONALD STOKES

The Natural History of Wild Shrubs and Vines

THE
BUTTERFLY
BOOK

An Easy Guide to Butterfly Gardening,
Identification, and Behavior

DONALD and LILLIAN STOKES
and ERNEST WILLIAMS

Little, Brown and Company

Boston   New York   Toronto   London

First Edition

Library of Congress Cataloging-in-Publication Data
Stokes, Donald W.
  The butterfly book: an easy guide to butterfly gardening, identification, and behavior / Donald and Lillian Stokes and Ernest Williams. — 1st ed.
      p.   cm.
    ISBN 0-316-81780-5
    1. Butterflies — North America — Identification.
2. Butterfly gardening.   3. Butterflies — Behavior.
I. Stokes, Lillian Q.   II. Williams, Ernest.   III. Title.
    QL548.S76   1991
    595.78′9097 — dc20   91-15323

10 9 8 7 6 5 4

RRD-OH

Published simultaneously in Canada by Little, Brown & Company (Canada) Limited

Printed in the United States of America

Photograph Acknowledgments
Kathleen and Lindsey Brown: 6, 20, 24, 33, 35 (spicebush swallowtail), 47 top, 59 left, 61 right, 66, 79, 84, 85, 86, 87.
Alan Charnley: 1, 23 (pupa just before adult emerges), 25, 27, 35 (black swallowtail), 45 bottom, 48 bottom, 54, 61 left, 63 right, 64, 65 left, 74 bottom, 76, 80.
Raymond Coleman: 17 (butterfly weed), 21 (black swallowtail), 34 (zebra, Baltimore, question mark, American painted lady, painted lady), 35 (giant swallowtail, tiger swallowtail, zebra swallowtail, silver-spotted skipper, long-tailed skipper), 46, 67, 69 top, 78.
William Davies: 17 (butterfly bush), 34 (gulf fritillary, comma), 35 (pipevine swallowtail, anise swallowtail, gray hairstreak), 48 top, 53, 55, 58, 74 top, 75, 82 bottom, 83, 93.
Pearl Eslinger: 19, 34 (great spangled fritillary).
John Fowler/Valan Photos: 35 (cabbage white, eyed brown), 50, 62.
Jon K. Hudgens: 94.
Steve Prchal/Sonoran Arthropod Studies, Inc.: 21 (cloudless sulphur, Milbert's tortoiseshell, red-spotted purple), 34 (mourning cloak, Milbert's tortoiseshell, buckeye), 35 (dog face), 71, 72, 90.
Jane Ruffin: 16 (Joe-Pye weed), 23 (top row, emerged adult, drying adult), 69 bottom.
John Shaw: 49, 56 right, 59 right, 60, 63 left, 92.
Leroy Simon: 7, 30, 45 top, 68, 70, 81 top, 82 top, 95.
Bob Simpson: 47 bottom.
Stokes Nature Company: 8, 16 (black-eyed Susan, liatris, coreopsis), 17 (New England aster, purple coneflower).
Stanley Temple: 77.
John Tveten: 21 (queen, banded hairstreak), 23 (pupa), 26, 28, 34 (West Coast lady, red admiral, white admiral, viceroy, red-spotted purple), 35 (checkered white, falcate orange tip, cloudless sulphur, banded hairstreak, monarch, queen, tawny emperor), 44, 51, 52, 56 left, 57, 65 right, 81 bottom, 88.
Tom Tyning: 29, 89, 91.
Ernest Williams: 37, 38, 39, 40, 41, 42.
Bob Wilson: 9, 16 (pentas), 17 (lantana), 18, 31, 73.
Mark Wilson: 10.

Garden Plans by Stokes Nature Company.
Species Icons by Ernest Williams.

Contents

ENJOYING BUTTERFLIES

Butter Flying?

Butterflies, alighting on one flower and then the next, have long fascinated and delighted humans with their gorgeous colors. One story has it that their English name originated in Britain, where people likened the yellow brimstone butterflies seen fluttering in woodlands in early spring to butter flying.

The astounding transformation of butterflies from earthbound caterpillars to winged adults has repeatedly captured people's imagination. But it was not until the last few hundred years that people even suspected there was a connection between

A monarch butterfly taking a moment to sip nectar from a loosestrife flower.

the two. Early naturalists thought that butterflies and caterpillars were separate kinds of creatures. Pliny the Elder, the Roman naturalist, thought caterpillars came from the morning dew that formed on tree leaves, and for many centuries this was accepted as fact.

Backyard Sanctuary

A wonderful feature of butterflies is that you can easily attract them to your backyard. All you need to do is provide plants on which the caterpillars can feed and flowers from which the adults can sip nectar. This will not only attract the butterflies for your own enjoyment but also help them flourish. Thus, butterflies are something you can help to conserve through the actions you take right in your own backyard.

Butterfly Conservation

With growing environmental awareness, people now realize that butterflies need to be conserved. Many species are endangered and others are less plentiful than they used to be even a few decades ago. Butterflies, like plants and other animals, are important to the survival of all living things. To a limited extent they pollinate flowers. They also play a part in the food web; the larvae eat leaves and in turn are eaten by many birds, amphibians, and reptiles. In addition, it would be a great sorrow to lose creatures that are so beautiful.

Because of this, there are many conservation organizations monitoring and trying to protect butterfly populations. There is even a Fourth of July Count, much like the Christmas Count for birds, in which butterfly species and numbers are tallied each year in designated areas. These

A lovely tiger swallowtail, one of the prettiest butterflies likely to visit your butterfly garden.

counts help determine which butterfly populations are scarce or declining.

Cameras, Not Collections

A common pastime for many decades has been collecting butterflies, killing them, and mounting them in boxes. Collections are still very important to scientific studies of butterfly species, populations, and behavior. But for the general public, it is far better to enjoy butterflies in their living state. This is especially true at this time, when interest in butterflies is growing so fast.

We watch butterflies at flowers, where they are still and can be approached as they feed; we observe their behavior as they go about their daily activities; we use binoculars to watch the shier species from a distance, just as we would with birds; and sometimes we use a net to catch a butterfly, then identify it and release it.

Many people also love to draw or photograph butterflies. This is a wonderful way to enjoy their beauty and keep a record of what you see.

About This Book

We start this book with gardening, for this is how you can enrich your backyard habitat in a way that will attract butterflies and provide for their continuing needs. Following this are several chapters on the basics of butterfly lives — how they grow and act, and why they are so colorful. The next section is a field guide to the identification of the caterpillars and adults of the common backyard species in North America. And, finally, we cover in detail the life and behavior of each species, providing up-to-date information on many interesting scientific discoveries.

We hope this book will encourage those of you who love butterflies to help conserve them through the knowledge that you gain — knowledge of species, knowledge of behavior, and knowledge of the native plants that butterflies need. We like to think that butterflies and the plants and habitats on which they depend will someday be a part of everyone's backyard.

Don and Lillian Stokes and Ernest Williams

BUTTERFLY GARDENING: INITIAL PLANNING

Nature's Jewelry

One sunny day in late August, while we (Don and Lillian Stokes, that is) stood in our butterfly garden, twenty butterflies fluttered in the sunlight and floated from flower to flower sipping nectar. Alfalfa and clouded sulphurs, cabbage whites, monarchs, and a viceroy drank from the 'September Ruby' asters. Pearl crescents and various skippers visited the black-eyed Susans, while a red admiral landed on the marigolds. A beautiful great spangled fritillary fed on the mauve liatris, and an American painted lady landed next to it, sharing in the bounty.

As we walked, our feet scared up a diminutive

The abundance of asters and black-eyed Susans in our garden attracts many butterflies.

eastern tailed blue from the grasses and an elusive mourning cloak drifted out from the woodland shadows across the sunny green lawn. On some nearby Queen Anne's lace a black swallowtail laid her eggs. Our garden was so much richer because of the butterflies that decorated it. They were like a glittering array of nature's jewelry.

It was not by accident that all these butterflies were here. We had carefully planned this magical garden with just the right combination of butterfly attractants.

How to Create a Butterfly Garden

You too can have this wonderful experience of intermingling butterflies and flowers by planting a butterfly garden. This chapter and the two that follow will tell you all the tricks for making it a success. First, here are some basic principles for attracting butterflies.

Grow Lots of Nectar Plants

The main food of adult butterflies is nectar from flowers. As they gather nectar, they also inadvertently do some pollination. Certain flowers are more appealing to butterflies than others, and you will find photos and a list of recommended flowers in the next chapter under the headings Top Ten Nectar Plants and Butterfly Nectar Sources.

When planting flowers, group them together and they will be more enticing to butterflies. Given a choice among equally appealing flowers, butterflies usually choose those that are most abundant. One of our butterfly gardens is 40 feet by 6 feet and is filled with butterfly flowers, especially asters. On one clump of New England asters that is 4 feet in diameter we observed 12 butterflies feeding at the same time.

A beautiful zebra swallowtail butterfly on verbena.

Be sure that your garden offers nectaring flowers throughout the blooming season so that butterflies can always find food. Also, have nectar plants of various heights, for smaller species of butterflies often stay low, while larger species often prefer to stay high when feeding.

From a butterfly's point of view, you cannot have too many flowers. If acquiring lots of plants seems expensive, consider growing your plants from seed. Another good trick is to find a gardening friend who is dividing his or her perennials in spring, and see if he or she will give you some of the divisions.

Grow Caterpillar Food Plants

If you want even more butterflies in your garden, provide food for caterpillars (the larval stage of butterflies) as well; they require a different menu than adult butterflies. Caterpillars eat the leaves and sometimes flowers and seeds of certain plants. They are often highly selective in their tastes, and some species will eat only one species of plant. Thus, you need to provide specific plants for certain species of caterpillars.

It is actually the adult female butterfly that chooses these plants and then lays her eggs on them. So by planting larval food plants you will attract egg-laying females to your garden.

Many larval plants are wildflowers, weeds, and grasses that belong in an informal setting, not in a flower border. You may want to designate a separate area for these, away from the main flower garden. For a list of larval food plants, see page 19.

Choose a Sunny Location

Sun is extremely important for both butterflies and flowers. Butterflies need sun to keep their bodies warm enough so they can fly. Only when their body temperature is about 85–100°F can they fly well. When the air temperature is cooler than this, they bask in the sun to warm themselves to effective flight temperature. This is why on cloudy days you may not see butterflies at all, and why butterflies become inactive on a partly cloudy day when the sun is blocked by clouds; they are perching, waiting for the sun.

Being able to fly earlier and later in the day is extremely advantageous for butterflies. Males can feed more and have longer to look for mates; females have more time to feed and to lay eggs. Places with little sun may actually limit the number of eggs a female can lay by limiting the time available for egg laying. Sunny spots are also good for eggs and caterpillars, for warm habitats enable them to develop more rapidly — sometimes up to 50 percent faster. Thus, a sunny garden will not only attract more butterflies but may actually produce more butterflies as well.

Butterfly weed, shown here with two great spangled fritillaries, is irresistible to many butterflies.

You can help butterflies by providing some rocks or evergreens in your garden in spots that get sun early in the day. The rocks or evergreens will absorb the heat from the sun, and the butterflies can perch on them to bask, warm up, and start flying earlier.

As avid gardeners know, sun is also important to the flowers. Many perennials and other larval food plants grow best in full sun. The amount of nectar production in their flowers can be determined by the amount of light they receive. Also, in sun, larval food plants will provide more fresh leaves for hungry caterpillars.

Provide Shelter

A butterfly garden should be planted in a location that is sheltered from the wind. This helps butterflies in two ways: they are not cooled by breezes, and they do not have to expend extra energy fighting wind currents as they try to feed, mate, and lay eggs. Warm, protected, sunny places are particularly important to butterflies in spring and fall, when the nights are cooler and it might take them longer to heat up to a level at which they can fly.

Warm, sheltered areas will also help flowers.

Taller species will be protected from blowing over; many species will bloom earlier in spring; and others will continue blooming later in fall. This will extend the time that nectar is available, and your garden can then have butterflies for more months of the year.

Shelter can be provided by a row of shrubs or trees, especially evergreens, placed so as to protect the garden from prevailing winds. A fence or rock wall can also be effective.

Do Not Use Pesticides

Butterflies are insects, so pesticides that rid your garden of insect pests will also rid your garden of butterflies. This includes the use of the bacterial insecticide BT, *Bacillus thuringiensis*. It will kill butterfly larvae. There are many alternative, safe ways to control unwanted visitors. When necessary, we use our own homemade spray of soapsuds, garlic, chives, and Tabasco to control insects like aphids. We also have developed a tolerance for a chewed leaf or two; we would far rather have the butterflies and other insects than a spotless garden.

Butterfly Feeders and Other Attractions

People have made butterfly feeders out of test tubes decorated to look like flowers or hummingbird feeders filled with a 10 percent sugar-water solution. Plugging the test tubes with cotton creates a kind of wick that feeds the sugar solution to the top of the tube and helps retard evaporation. Butterfly feeders are commercially available. See Resources, page 96.

There are other things you can do to attract butterflies. Some butterflies like to drink from the wet edges of mud puddles or wet sandy areas. When doing this they are ingesting important minerals and nutrients needed for survival and reproduction. (See Puddling, Courting, Basking, Egg Laying, page 28.) Consider making a mud puddle in a corner of the garden, or fill a bowl with wet sand and sink it in the ground.

Some butterflies never feed on nectar; instead, they feed on rotting fruit, sap, and even dung, urine, and carrion, from which they get nutrients and minerals. You can put rotting fruit on trays

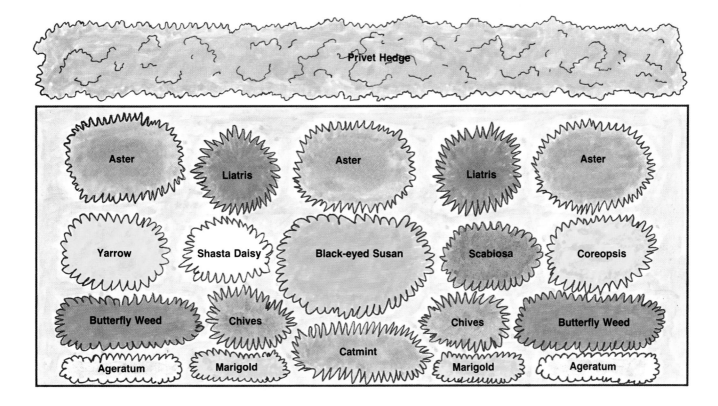

Garden Plan 1: A Small Butterfly Garden
Size of Bed: 5 feet × 12 feet

as a butterfly attractant, but be aware that other animals, such as raccoons, may also be drawn to it.

In addition to food, you can provide protected places for species that overwinter as adults. These butterflies hibernate in tree crevices, under bark, in log piles, or in the nooks of buildings. You can make a butterfly hibernation box from a wooden container 3 feet high, 6 inches wide, and 6 inches deep. Cut two long ¾-inch-wide slits in the front. Mount the box vertically on a tree and hinge the lid so you can look in to see if you have any wintering guests.

Garden Plans

For your butterfly garden, you can either start from scratch or add to an existing garden bed. Perhaps there already is a sheltered, sunny lo-

cation on your property that is dug up and has some plants. You can add butterfly plants to this area or exchange the existing plants for ones that are more favorable to butterflies.

We are including two garden plans (above and page 13) that you may wish to use, or you can create your own. When planning, bear in mind that shrubs go in the back, next the tallest flowers, then those of medium height, and finally the shortest ones in front. This provides a banked or stepped effect that enables you to see all the flowers. Choose a mixture of perennials and annuals. Annuals bloom all summer, whereas perennials have more limited blooming times. Perennials nevertheless are desirable because they bloom year after year from the same roots, while annuals must grow from seed each year. Make sure to have lots of plants from the Top Ten list, because they will attract the most butterflies.

BUTTERFLY GARDENING: NECTAR PLANTS

Butterfly Choice

Many flowers produce nectar, but butterflies clearly favor some over others. For example, butterfly bush and butterfly weed seem irresistible to butterflies and belong in every garden. To help you select plants for your butterfly garden, we have provided two lists. The Top Ten list on pages 16–17 includes ten of the most preferred butterfly attractants. The more extensive list on pages 14–15 includes many other plants that are known to attract butterflies.

These lists are by no means exhaustive; butterflies visit hundreds of plants. Since this is one of the least-studied aspects of butterfly behavior, we encourage you to experiment.

About the Nectar Plant Charts

Names — We have included the common names of the plants as well as their scientific names because they can be listed either way by nurseries. The abbreviation spp. indicates that more than one species in that genus of plants is attractive to butterflies.

Hardiness Zones — The zone given for each plant is the coldest hardiness zone where it will grow normally, but the plant can be expected to grow in the warmer zones as well. Hardiness zones for annuals are not listed, since annuals do not overwinter. Hardiness zones are based on the average minimum temperature of that region. See map on this page.

Height — Plant heights are often given as a range, because height can be affected by differing soil, moisture, and temperature conditions.

Color — A general rule of thumb for an appealing garden is to keep cool colors together and hot colors together. Some hot colors, such as reds and yellows, can be softened by adding cool blues or whites.

Bloom Times — Bloom times are indicated as early, mid, or late season. These are approximate and based on when the plants bloom in Zone 5.

Availability — We have listed annuals, perennials, trees, shrubs, and vines that are generally available from nurseries and plant catalogs. Some wildflowers may be hard to obtain because they are not sold in nurseries.

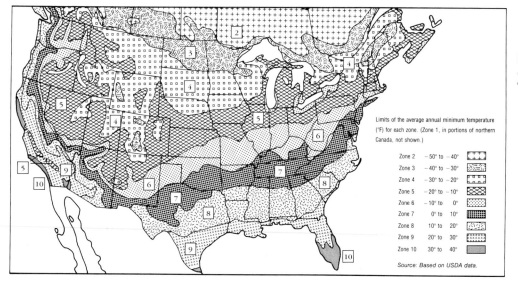

Plant Hardiness Zones

Limits of the average annual minimum temperature (°F) for each zone. (Zone 1, in portions of northern Canada, not shown.)

Zone 2	− 50° to − 40°
Zone 3	− 40° to − 30°
Zone 4	− 30° to − 20°
Zone 5	− 20° to − 10°
Zone 6	− 10° to 0°
Zone 7	0° to 10°
Zone 8	10° to 20°
Zone 9	20° to 30°
Zone 10	30° to 40°

Source: Based on USDA data.

Garden Plan 2: A Large Butterfly Garden
Scale: 1 inch = 5 feet

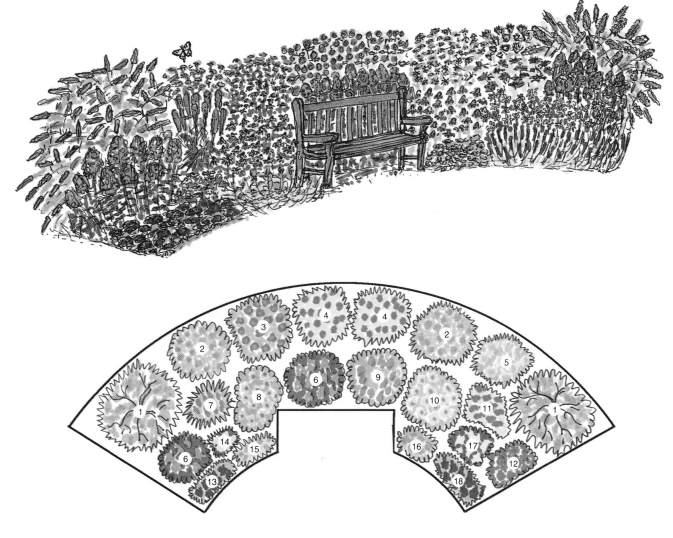

1. Butterfly bush (*Buddleia davidii*)
2. Aster (*Aster novae-angliae*)
3. Aster (*Aster* 'September Ruby')
4. Globe thistle (*Echinops exaltatus*)
5. Joe-Pye weed (*Eupatorium* spp.)
6. Phlox (*Phlox paniculata*)
7. Liatris (*Liatris* spp.)
8. Black-eyed Susan (*Rudbeckia fulgida speciosa* 'Goldstrum')
9. Phlox (*Phlox carolina* 'Rosalinde')
10. Purple coneflower (*Echinacea purpurea*)
11. Bee Balm (*Monarda didyma* 'Blue Stocking')
12. Phlox (*Phlox paniculata* 'Ann')
13. Heliotrope (*Heliotropium arborescens*)
14. Marigold (*Tagetes patula*)
15. Catmint (*Nepeta mussinii*)
16. Lantana (*Lantana camara*)
17. Coreopsis (*Coreopsis verticillata* 'Moonbeam')
18. Lavender (*Lavandula angustifolia* 'Hidcote Strain')

Butterfly Nectar Sources

Common Name (Scientific Name)	Zone	Height	Color
ANNUALS			
Ageratum (*Ageratum houstonianum*)		6–8 in.	purple
Cosmos (*Cosmos bipinnatus*), 'Sensation'		3 ft.	pink, whites
Heliotrope (*Heliotropium arborescens*)		1 ft.	purple
Lantana (*Lantana camara*)		1–3 ft.	red, yellow, blue
Lunaria, honesty (*Lunaria annua*) — sometimes biennial		2–3 ft.	purple, white
Marigold, French marigold (*Tagetes patula*)		1 ft.	yellow, orange
Mexican sunflower (*Tithonia rotundifolia*)		3–5 ft.	yellow, orange
Nicotiana, flowering tobacco (*Nicotiana alata*)		2 ft.	pinks, whites
Pentas (*Pentas lanceolata*) — subshrub		1½ ft.	purple, rose, white
Petunia (*Petunia* x *hybrida*)		1 ft.	pink, white, blue
Scabiosa, pincushion flower (*Scabiosa atropurpurea*)		1½ ft.	blue
Statice (*Limonium sinuatum*)		1–1½ ft.	purple, blue
Verbena (*Verbena* x *hortensis*, *V.* x *hybrida*)		1 ft.	rose, pink
Zinnia (*Zinnia elegans*)		1–2 ft.	pinks, yellows, rose
PERENNIALS			
Early			
Allium (*Allium* spp.) — bulb	3	2–4 ft.	purple
Arabis (*Arabis albida*)	4	6 in.	white
Aubrieta, purple rock cress (*Aubrieta deltoidea*)	4	3–6 in.	purple
Chives (*Allium schoenoprasum*)	2	2 ft.	purple
Dame's rocket (*Hesperis matronalis*)	3	2–3½ ft.	purple, sometimes pink, white
Forget-me-not (*Myosotis sylvatica*) — biennial, perennial	3	9–24 in.	blue
Midseason			
Bee balm (*Monarda didyma*)	4	3 ft.	pink, red
Black-eyed Susan, gloriosa daisy (*Rudbeckia* spp.) — biennial, perennial	3	3 ft.	yellow
Butterfly weed (*Asclepias tuberosa*)	3	2–3 ft.	orange
Catmint (*Nepeta mussinii*)	4	1 ft.	blue-purple
Coreopsis (*Coreopsis* spp.)	3	2 ft.	yellow
Daisy, shasta daisy (*Chrysanthemum maximum, C.* x *superbum*)	4	2–3 ft.	white
Daylily (*Hemerocallis* spp.)	2	2–3 ft.	yellow, orange, peach, pink
Erigeron, fleabane (*Erigeron speciosus*)	2	1–3 ft.	lavender-blue
Gaillardia, blanket flower (*Gaillardia* x *grandiflora*)	2	1–3 ft.	yellow and red
Lavender (*Lavandula angustifolia*)	5	1–3 ft.	purple
Liatris, blazing-star, gay-feather (*Liatris* spp.)	2	2–4 ft.	mauve
Lily (*Lilium* spp.)	3	2–5 ft.	yellow, pink, white, red
Loosestrife (*Lythrum virgatum*), 'Morden's Gleam'	3	3–4 ft.	pink
Mint (*Mentha* spp.)	3	1–4 ft.	purple, white
Phlox (*Phlox* spp.)	4	3 ft.	pink, white, rose, blue, mauve
Purple coneflower (*Echinacea purpurea*)	3	2–3 ft.	pink, white
Red valerian (*Centranthus ruber*)	4	2–3 ft.	deep rose
Rosemary (*Rosemarinus officinalis*) — subshrub	6	2–6 ft.	violet-blue
Sunflower (*Helianthus* spp.)	3	3–5 ft.	yellow
Veronica (*Veronica* spp.)	5	6–18 in.	blue, pink
Yarrow (*Achillea filipendulina*), 'Coronation Gold'	2	2–3 ft.	yellow
Late			
Aster, Michaelmas daisy (*Aster* spp.)	2	3–5 ft.	purple, ruby, pink, blue
Globe thistle (*Echinops exaltatus*)	3	2–4 ft.	purple
Physostegia, obedient plant (*Physostegia virginiana*)	2	2½–4 ft.	pink
Sedum, showy sedum (*Sedum spectabile vulgaris*)	3	1–1½ ft.	pink
Sneezeweed (*Helenium autumnale*)	3	4–6 ft.	yellow, orange

Common Name (Scientific Name)	Zone	Height	Color
WILDFLOWERS			
Early			
Clover (*Trifolium* spp.)	3	4–8 in.	pink, white
Dandelion (*Taraxacum officinale*)	3	6–8 in.	yellow
Hawkweed (*Hieracium* spp.)	3	6–12 in.	yellow, orange
Winter cress (*Barbarea* spp.)	3	1–1½ ft.	yellow
Midseason			
Butterfly weed (*Asclepias tuberosa*)	3	1–2 ft.	orange
Daisy, Oxeye daisy (*Chrysanthemum leucanthemum*)	3	1–2 ft.	white
Dogbane (*Apocynum androsaemifolium*)	3	1–2 ft.	pink
Milkweed (*Asclepias* spp.)	3	3 ft.	pink
Mountain mint (*Pycnanthemum* spp.)	2	1–2½ ft.	white
Pearly everlasting (*Anaphalis margaritacea*)	3	1–3 ft.	white
Queen Anne's lace (*Daucus carota*)	3	3–3½ ft.	white
Thistle (*Cirsium* spp.)	3	3–4 ft.	purple
Vetch (*Vicia* spp.)	3	6 ft.	purple
Wild bergamot (*Monarda fistulosa*)	3	3–4 ft.	lavender
Yarrow (*Achillea millefolium*)	2	2 ft.	white
Late			
Aster (*Aster* spp., especially *A. novae-angliae*)	3	4 ft.	purple-blue
Beggar ticks (*Bidens aristosa*)	4	1–3 ft.	yellow
Boneset (*Eupatorium perfoliatum*)	3	4–5 ft.	white
Goldenrod (*Solidago* spp.)	3	3 ft.	yellow
Ironweed (*Vernonia* spp.)	4	3–7 ft.	purple
Joe-Pye weed (*Eupatorium* spp.)	2	5–9 ft.	pinkish purple
SHRUBS			
Early			
Lilac (*Syringa vulgaris*)	3	20 ft.	purple, pink, white
Rhododendron (*Rhododendron* spp.)	4	to 18 ft.	pink, purple, white
Spicebush (*Lindera benzoin*)	4	15 ft.	yellow
Midseason			
Butterfly bush (*Buddleia davidii*, *B. alternifolia*)	5	6–15 ft.	purple
Buttonbush (*Cephalanthus occidentalis*)	4	15 ft.	white
Flame-of-the-woods (*Ixora coccinea*)	10	15 ft.	red and yellow
Honeysuckle shrub (*Lonicera tatarica*)	3	9 ft.	pale pink
New Jersey tea (*Ceanothus americanus*)	4	3 ft.	white
Privet: Amur privet (*Ligustrum amurense*) in North	3	15 ft.	white
California privet (*L. ovalifolium*) in Calif.	6	15 ft.	white
Japanese privet (*L. japonicum*) in South	7	6–18 ft.	white
Sweet pepperbush, summer sweet (*Clethra alnifolia*)	3	4–6 ft.	white
Late			
Bluebeard (*Caryopteris* x *clandonensis*)	5	2–4 ft.	blue
Glossy abelia (*Abelia* x *grandiflora*)	5	5 ft.	pink
Sweet pepperbush (*Clethra arborea*)	9	25 ft.	white
TREES			
Buckeye (*Aesculus* spp.)	3	75 ft.	white, greenish yellow, pink
Japanese Tree Lilac (*Syringa reticulata*)	4	30 ft.	white
Plum, cherry (*Prunus* spp.)	3	20–30 ft.	pink
Willow (*Salix* spp.)	2	10–45 ft.	greenish yellow
VINES			
Japanese honeysuckle (*Lonicera japonica*)	4	vine	white

BUTTERFLY GARDENING: LARVAL FOOD PLANTS

Working with Your Environment

Butterfly larval food plants span the gamut from beautiful garden perennials, to vegetables, to wildflowers, to weeds. They also include many trees and shrubs. Because of this, larval food plant gardening is different from nectar plant gardening. Rather than involving planning a formal garden, it is more a process of knowing the best larval plants and encouraging their growth on your property, wherever they happen to be.

When choosing larval food plants, remember to check the distributional range of the butterflies you are trying to attract. (Use the range maps in the second half of this book.) If you are out of a butterfly's range, you cannot attract it. For the common butterflies covered in this book, there are only a few plants that attract three or more species for egg laying. Two related trees are at the top of this list — quaking aspen and common cottonwood. Ten butterfly species featured in this book and several others as well commonly lay their eggs on these trees. The next most popular larval food plant is hackberry, which attracts five species. Other plants that attract three or more species include clover, alfalfa, vetch, winter cress, willow, cabbage, false nettle, and nettle. Most nettles have irritating spines and should not be handled.

Try pruning the tips of these plants or others, such as milkweed, to produce new leaves, which caterpillars prefer. Larval plants that are weedy can be put in pots to prevent their spreading, and then placed in your garden. Many other tips on how to use larval food plants are mentioned in the box labeled How to Attract in each of the chapters on butterflies.

How to Get Plants

How you obtain larval food plants varies with the type of plant. Many flowers, shrubs, and trees can obviously be bought in nurseries. Vegetable plants can be bought as seedlings or seeds.

Plants that are generally considered weeds can often be encouraged simply by turning over the soil in an area and leaving it alone. For others, look for them growing naturally, try to gather some seeds, and scatter them over bare earth.

Some plants that are considered wildflowers, such as milkweed, everlasting, asters, turtlehead, and lupine, should not be dug out of wild areas. It is better to try to acquire these plants from native plant societies that propagate them.

Two zebra swallowtails mating.

Primary Larval Food Plants and the Butterflies That Use Them

Plant	Butterflies
Alfalfa (*Medicago sativa*) F	Clouded sulphur, alfalfa sulphur, eastern tailed blue
Aspen, cottonwood (*Populus* spp.) T	White admiral, red-spotted purple, western admiral, Lorquin's admiral, viceroy, mourning cloak, tiger swallowtail, western tiger swallowtail
Aster (*Aster* spp.) F	Pearl crescent
Bean (*Phaseolus* spp.) V	Long-tailed skipper
Birch (*Betula* spp.) T	Mourning cloak, white admiral
Blueberry (*Vaccinium* spp.) S	Brown elfin
Cabbage, broccoli (*Brassica* spp.) V	Cabbage white, checkered white
Cherry (*Prunus* spp.) T, S	Red-spotted purple, tiger swallowtail, spring azure
Citrus trees (*Citrus* spp.) T	Anise swallowtail, giant swallowtail
Clover (*Trifolium* spp.) F	Clouded sulphur, alfalfa sulphur, eastern tailed blue
Dogwood (*Cornus* spp.) T, S	Spring azure
Elm (*Ulmus* spp.) T	Comma, question mark, mourning cloak
Everlasting (*Gnaphalium* spp.) F	American painted lady
False indigo (*Amorpha* spp.) S	Dog face, silver-spotted skipper
False nettle (*Boehmeria cylindrica*) F	Red admiral, question mark, comma, Milbert's tortoiseshell
Grasses, sedges (various genera)	Common wood nymph, little wood satyr, eyed brown, ringlet, fiery skipper, European skipper
Hackberry (*Celtis* spp.) T	Question mark, comma, hackberry butterfly, tawny emperor, snout butterfly, mourning cloak
Hops (*Humulus lupulus*) F	Question mark, comma
Knotweed (*Polygonum* spp.) F	Purplish copper
Locust (*Robinia* spp.) T, S	Silver-spotted skipper
Lupine (*Lupinus* spp.) F	Silvery blue, other blues
Mallow (*Malva* spp.) F	West Coast lady, gray hairstreak
Marigold (*Tagetes* spp.) F	Dainty sulphur
Meadowsweet (*Spiraea* spp.) S	Spring azure
Milk vetch (*Astragalus* spp.) F	Western tailed blue, other blues
Milkweed (*Asclepias* spp.) F	Monarch, queen
Nettle (*Urtica* spp.) F	Red admiral, question mark, comma, Milbert's tortoiseshell
Oak (*Quercus* spp.) T, S	Sister, banded hairstreak
Parsley (*Petroselinum crispum*) V	Black swallowtail, anise swallowtail
Passionflower (*Passiflora* spp.) F	Gulf fritillary, zebra
Pawpaw (*Asimina* spp.) T	Zebra swallowtail
Pipevine (*Aristolochia* spp.) F	Pipevine swallowtail
Plantain (*Plantago* spp.) F	Buckeye, Baltimore
Queen Anne's lace (*Daucus carota*) F	Black swallowtail, anise swallowtail
Senna (*Cassia* spp.) F	Cloudless sulphur
Snapdragon (*Antirrhinum* spp.) F	Buckeye
Sneezeweed (*Helenium* spp.) F	Dainty sulphur
Sorrel, dock (*Rumex* spp.) F	American copper, purplish copper
Spicebush, sassafras (*Lindera* spp.) S	Spicebush swallowtail, tiger swallowtail
Stonecrop (*Sedum* spp.) F	Phoebus parnassian
Sweet fennel (*Foeniculum vulgare*) F	Anise swallowtail, black swallowtail
Thistle (*Cirsium* spp.) F	Painted lady
Tulip poplar (*Liriodendron tulipifera*) T	Tiger swallowtail
Turtlehead (*Chelone* spp.) F	Baltimore, buckeye
Vetch (*Vicia* spp.) F	Alfalfa sulphur, eastern tailed blue, western tailed blue, other blues
Violet (*Viola* spp.) F	Great spangled fritillary, meadow fritillary, other fritillaries
Willow (*Salix* spp.) T, S	Western admiral, Lorquin's admiral, viceroy, mourning cloak, western tiger swallowtail
Winter cress (*Barbarea* spp.) F	Sara orange tip, falcate orange tip, cabbage white

A black swallowtail caterpillar feeds on Queen Anne's lace.

T = tree, S = shrub, F = flower, V = vegetable

THE LIFE STAGES OF A BUTTERFLY

What Is a Butterfly?

Butterflies are a type of insect. Insects are distinguished from all other animals by having an external skeleton (a hard outer covering), three main body parts (head, thorax, and abdomen), and three pairs of jointed legs (all attached to the thorax).

Butterflies are closely related to skippers and the many kinds of moths, and all belong to the order of insects called Lepidoptera, which means "scaly wings." The thousands of little scales on their wings distinguish moths, butterflies, and skippers from all other flying insects.

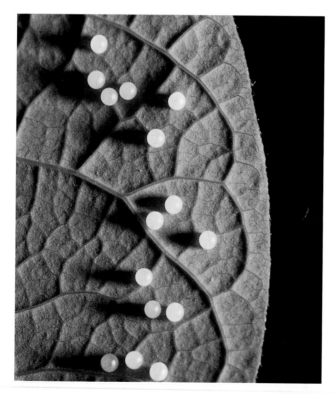

The eggs of a spicebush swallowtail on spicebush. Usually, there are fewer eggs on a single leaf.

The most reliable way to distinguish among butterflies, skippers, and moths is by their antennae: butterflies have clubbed antennae (swollen at the tip); skippers have clubbed antennae with a point at the tip; and moths have feathered or filamentous antennae. In addition, butterflies and skippers have slender bodies and are daytime fliers, whereas the vast majority of moths have heavier bodies and fly at night.

The Stages of Life

There are four stages to a butterfly's life, and each is radically different from the others. Briefly, a butterfly starts as an egg, which hatches in about 5 to 10 days. The tiny caterpillar starts to eat and, as it gets bigger, sheds its skin 4 to 6 times. After about 2 to 4 weeks it is full grown and transforms into a pupa, a quiescent stage during which its body structures change into those of an adult. Ten to fifteen days later the adult butterfly emerges. Adults mate, the females lay eggs, and the cycle starts over.

This whole process is called metamorphosis, which means "change of form."

Butterfly Eggs

Individual female butterflies can lay up to 1,600 eggs in the course of their life. Eggs are laid with a covering that glues them to the leaf or twig where they are placed and then hardens to form a protective, waterproof shell. Most butterflies lay their eggs singly. A few, such as the mourning cloak, question mark, comma, Baltimore, tawny emperor, and pearl crescent, lay eggs in clusters.

The time eggs take to hatch depends on several variables. The most important is temperature. An average difference of just 15° F can cause eggs to

The pupae of various butterflies with clues to family characteristics (clockwise from upper left): Black swallowtail — swallowtail pupae point up, have girdle of silk, two prominent points at front end. Cloudless sulphur — sulphur and white pupae point up, have girdle of silk, single point at front end. Queen (monarch similar) — pupae hang down, are smooth, green with brown-gold dots. Milbert's tortoiseshell and (next photo) red-spotted purple — brush-footed pupae hang down, have lots of projections. Banded hairstreak — gossamer wing pupae are small, rounded, have girdle of silk.

develop up to 4 times faster, hatching in just 3 days instead of 12.

Butterfly eggs vary in shape and texture. For example, swallowtail eggs are smooth spheres with a flattened base, whereas the eggs of whites and sulphurs are long and thin. Eggs also vary in size among species and during the life of individuals — eggs laid by older females may be smaller, possibly due to depleted nutritional reserves.

Color is another variable. Eggs of the monarch are green, those of black swallowtails are pale yellow, whereas those of metalmarks are pink. The eggs of the clouded sulphur start pale yellow and then change to red; those of wood nymphs start yellow and within the first day turn brown. Most butterfly eggs also become darker just before the caterpillar hatches.

Caterpillar Life

A caterpillar's first meal is often its own eggshell, and then it feeds on its food plant. At first the caterpillar is so tiny it can only scrape at the leaf surface, sometimes creating small holes. When larger, it aligns itself along the leaf edge and eats chunks of leaf. Most caterpillars feed on the leaves of their food plants. The caterpillars of blues usually feed on flower buds or seeds, and those of the harvester butterfly (*Feniseca tarquinius*), our only carnivorous butterfly larvae, feed on aphids.

Most caterpillars alternate periods of feeding and resting during the day, but some, such as those of fritillaries, almost always feed at night. During the day they stay in leaf litter at the base of their food plants, which are violets.

Next time you get a chance, take a close look at a caterpillar. You will notice that it has a hardened head. There are six minute, simple eyes on each side that are limited to seeing light and shade and some movement. On the lower jaw are tiny spinnerets used to make silk.

Just behind the head on the underside of the caterpillar are three pairs of hardened legs used mostly for holding and manipulating food. Behind these are five pairs of soft, fleshy legs, called prolegs, that are used primarily for locomotion. When a caterpillar moves, it lifts one set of prolegs at a time, not lifting the second pair until the first pair is down. The feet are tipped with small hooks.

Although a caterpillar looks soft, its skin is quite inelastic. Because of this, it must molt its skin periodically as it grows. This takes a day or two and starts with the caterpillar's laying down a pad of silk and then grabbing hold of it with its prolegs. Thus secured, it then produces a second layer of skin under the old one, the two being separated by a thin layer of fluid. When the new skin is fully developed, the caterpillar starts to swallow air, which expands its body and splits open the old skin. After emerging, it waits to let its head and new skin harden before it resumes moving and eating. Most butterfly caterpillars molt 4 to 6 times, each stage between molts being called an instar. After its last molt it is a pupa.

The rate at which a caterpillar grows increases with each molt, for as it gets larger it can eat greater quantities of food. How large a caterpillar becomes in its last instar can determine the size of the adult butterfly. If the caterpillar runs out of food or is not able to eat due to bad weather, it will pupate early and be a slightly smaller adult. If it has abundant food, it may eat longer and become a larger adult. This is why adult butterflies of the same species can vary so much in size.

When finished growing, the caterpillar looks for a place in which to pupate. In summer this is often near the food plant, but in winter it may crawl to a more protected spot, such as leaf litter, a log pile, or someplace similar. Caterpillars that wander away from food plants to pupate may change color to brown, making them more camouflaged from predators. This is the case with the tiger swallowtail, which is green until pupation.

The Pupa, or Chrysalis

Once a caterpillar has found a good location to pupate, it makes preparations for the change. The first is to attach itself to a plant or other object. To do this it weaves a patch of silk there and then grabs hold of the silk with its rear prolegs. Depending on the species, it may hang upside down from this pad, or it may spin a thin girdle of silk that supports it in an upward position. Some, such as most of the skippers, pupate inside a thin covering of silk, often in among a few leaves tied loosely together.

The caterpillar may remain still for about a day as the pupal skin forms under the caterpillar skin. Then the old caterpillar skin splits open and the pupa emerges. First, the end of the pupa, which has hooks on it and is called the cremaster, breaks through the larval skin. The cremaster is moved around until the hooks can catch onto the silken pad spun by the caterpillar. Now the pupa is free of the old skin and may actually wiggle around until the old skin drops off.

Pupae of some species can be either green or brown. One way this is controlled is by the color of the pupation site. If the caterpillar sees green, then the pupa is green; if it sees brown, then it turns brown. In summer pupae may be either green or brown. In winter, all pupae are brown. Obviously, color helps camouflage the pupa.

Just after emerging from the caterpillar skin, the pupa is particularly vulnerable to parasites that try to lay their eggs within it. This is because its skin is still soft. Later, the skin gradually hardens and is difficult to penetrate; the pupa may have a slippery surface that makes it difficult for larger parasites to hold onto. The pupa has several other defenses. Some can move when touched by parasites to startle and dislodge them, and others have sharp edges between abdominal segments which can close on parasites trying to penetrate between the segments.

Inside the pupal case, the caterpillar is transformed into an adult. Since hatching, the caterpillar contained growth centers called imaginal buds. These were inhibited from developing by the secretion of a juvenile hormone in the caterpillar from glands near the head. When production of this hormone is shut off in the last stage of caterpillar life, the caterpillar enters the pupal phase, and these imaginal buds begin to grow and develop into adult organs and structures. At the same time, many organs and structures of the caterpillar are dissolved into a juicy substance that feeds the growth of the adult structures. All of this takes about two weeks or a little less if conditions are ideal, such as the weather being warm.

Just before the adult emerges, the pupal case may become transparent and reveal the butterfly within.

The various life stages of a butterfly as shown in a monarch. Top row, left to right: egg; larva or caterpillar eating; larva transforming into a pupa, or chrysalis; pupa just before it hardens. Bottom row, left to right: pupa; pupa just before the adult emerges; emerged adult expanding its wings; adult drying its wings before its first flight.

Adult Butterfly

The pupal skin splits open near the head, and the adult butterfly crawls out with its wings all folded up. It moves to where it has room to hang upside down by its legs. The adult swallows air, which helps to pump fluid into the veins of the wings and make them expand to their full extent. It expels all the wastes accumulated during pupation in a drop or two of colored fluid, called the meconium. The butterfly remains still until the wings harden, and then it can fly.

The Cycle Continues

A complete life cycle of a butterfly population is called a brood. Some species have just one brood a year, others may have four or five. The same species can have many broods per year in the South and only one or two in the North due to the shorter season and cooler weather.

In the far South, some species remain active throughout winter, but in the North it is too cold and they stop all activity, in a hibernation-like period of dormancy called diapause. Each species usually has a fixed life stage in which it overwinters. For example, mourning cloaks overwinter as adults, most blues overwinter as pupae, and viceroys overwinter as caterpillars. Very few butterflies overwinter as eggs. The life cycle of each species is synchronized with the seasons so that most individuals of a brood will reach the proper stage when the weather gets cold.

Because of this, the length of any given life stage can vary, depending on whether it occurs in summer or winter. Most adult butterflies live only about two weeks in the summer, but if they overwinter as adults, then their lifespan can be many months.

You might wonder how butterflies survive freezing temperatures. This is generally accomplished in two ways. One is that they accumulate sugar in their blood, which acts like antifreeze in their bodies. Also, water within cells may move outside the cells so that when it freezes it does not harm the cell membranes.

Most butterflies winter in the same areas that they summer. But some southern butterflies, like the dainty sulphur, have populations which emigrate north each summer and then die out in winter, replaced by others from the south the next summer. Other butterflies, such as monarchs, move south in fall to avoid the cold.

BUTTERFLY COLORS

The Eye of the Beholder

As beautiful as the colors of butterfly wings are to us, they are probably even more striking to other butterflies. This is because adult butterflies see a larger spectrum of colors than many other animals. They can see all of the colors that we see and, in addition, they see ultraviolet colors.

Although butterflies see more colors than we do, other aspects of their vision are not as good as

Besides the beautiful colors that we see on butterflies and flowers, there are also ultraviolet colors, which the butterflies, like this gulf fritillary, can see.

ours. For example, they cannot see detail from a distance and so cannot recognize the fine patterns of other butterflies except from up close.

Ultraviolet colors are important to butterflies in sexual communication and in gathering food. Ultraviolet colors often are the distinguishing feature between males and females of a species or between species. For example, in many whites and sulphurs, the sexes look similar to us but in fact the males have much more ultraviolet reflectance.

There are also ultraviolet colors in many of the flowers from which butterflies get nectar. Because the surrounding green vegetation absorbs ultraviolet light, the ultraviolet colors of flowers stand out even more. Ultraviolet colors on flowers may also help direct butterflies and other insects to the nectar. The common daisy, for instance, looks just white and yellow to us but has ultraviolet colors right outside the yellow center.

Vertebrate predators on butterflies, such as birds, reptiles, and amphibians, do not see ultraviolet colors. Thus, ultraviolet colors are like a secret language for butterflies and some other insects.

Scales

Butterfly wings are clear but covered with tiny scales, each the outgrowth of a single cell. There are about 500 scales to the inch and about 125,000 per square inch. As you probably know if you have ever handled a butterfly or moth, the scales easily rub off the wings. Scales also come off during natural flight, and this is why older butterflies look more worn than ones that have freshly emerged from the pupae.

In addition to creating color patterns, scales serve several other functions: they aid in absorb-

The black swallowtail gains some protection from predators by looking like the distasteful pipevine swallowtail.

This close-up view of a giant swallowtail wing shows some of the structure of individual scales.

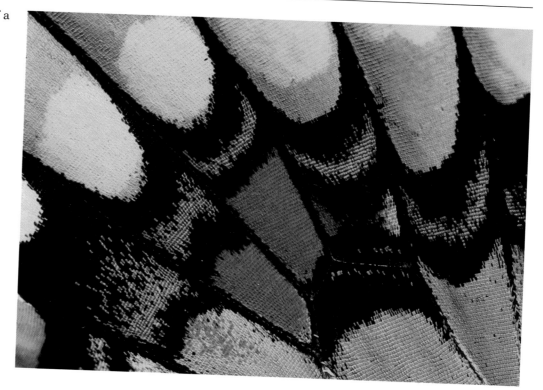

Mimicry

In whites, it is advanta
taste bad to look simila
tastes one member of a
avoid all of the rest. Th
monarch and the queen
that are both bad tastir

In a sense, they min
efit. This type of mimic
tasting butterflies look
mimicry, after Fritz M
phenomenon.

In other cases, g
evolved to look like bad
from the deception by
quently avoid them. C
tails, in which the
pipevine swallowtail, a
include the female bla
of the female eastern
spicebush swallowtail
viceroy butterfly as v
the monarch in north
form in Florida, whe
butterfly.

This type of mim
and bad-tasting speci

ing or reflecting sunlight during basking; their slipperiness and easy detachment may help butterflies escape predators; and some specialized scales, belonging mostly to males, produce scents during courtship.

The beautiful colors of scales are created in two ways — through pigments and through structure. The two main pigments of butterfly scales are melanins and pterins. Melanins create black, brown, tan, brownish red, and dark yellow; pterins create orange, yellow, red, and sometimes white.

All other colors of butterflies are created by structures in the scales that break up light through diffraction and interference. Iridescence, metallic colors, blues, greens, and even some whites are created in this way. The white "eyespots" on the wings of many butterflies are created by clear scales that contain pockets of air; the surfaces of these scales reflect and scatter light, making them look white. (Snow looks white for the same reason.) Some iridescent scales contain some melanins as well, which adds to their brilliance. Structural colors are often seen only from certain angles, and their effect may be intensified as the butterfly closes and opens its wings in flight.

Ultraviolet colors can be created both by pigments and by the structure of the scale.

Top Versus Bottom

In many of our common butterflies, the upper surface of the wings is more brightly colored than the undersurface. This is true of the American copper, spring azure, question mark, and meadow fritillary, to name a few. In these species, the upper surface is used to communicate with other butterflies and the undersurface hides the butterfly from predators. For example, the undersurface of the question mark's wings looks like tree bark or leaves, which is where this butterfly often rests. Colors that help animals hide are called cryptic colors.

Another interesting example of different under- and upper surfaces can be seen in the mourning cloak. Its upper surface has a bright yellow band along the outer edge, but its undersurface looks just like tree bark. As you watch the mourning cloak in flight, your eye keys in on the yellow. When the butterfly suddenly stops, your eye tends to keep moving, looking for the yellow. It takes a second or two to realize that the butterfly has landed, and by that time it has closed its wings and blended in perfectly with tree bark.

The banded hairst[...]
them that mimic [...]
predator to peck t[...]
escape.

Female and [...]

In some butterf[...]
in appearance [...]
white male ha[...]
whereas the fe[...]
tailed blue is [...]
bright blue; an[...]
bright yellow [...]
smaller dots. It [...]
that the femal[...]
that they are n[...]
they go about [...]

As noted, e[...]
male and fema[...]
differences in t[...]
they reflect, n[...]
females. It is [...]
eyes see only [...]
butterfly color[...]

PUDDLING, COURTING, BASKING, EGG LAYING

Four Behaviors That You Can Watch

Everybody knows that butterflies are beautiful, but few people know how interesting they are to watch as well. This chapter presents four fascinating behaviors of butterflies that you can easily observe wherever these lovely insects are active.

Puddling

Have you ever seen several butterflies all gathered around a puddle or damp place? This is a common behavior called puddling.

Puddling sites are often along dirt roads or paths through fields, where water regularly accumulates and then evaporates, thus concentrating minerals. Butterflies visit these sites, even after the puddles have dried up, for they are able to exude saliva through their proboscis and then suck it back up along with the nutrients.

Interestingly, almost all butterflies at puddling sites are males. Tests have shown that the most attractive element to males at puddling sites is sodium, a component of salt. Males need extra salt and other nutrients, such as amino acids, for mating (especially second matings). Males pass along nutrients with their sperm in a package called a spermatophore. These added nutrients, especially sodium, may aid the female in producing eggs. It may also be that nutrients gained from puddling are important in producing male scent (pheromone), which is used in courtship to attract females.

Sodium is important to the health and functioning of animals, but plants contain very little. Therefore, animals that eat only plants, such as deer or butterflies, need extra sodium to supple-

Two pipevine swallowtails mating.

ment this lack in their diet. This is why deer are attracted to salt licks.

Male butterflies are also attracted to carrion and animal scats, from which they probably also get important nutrients. They seem particularly attracted to the scats of carnivores, such as fox or coyote, possibly because these contain more salts or amino acids. In addition, they puddle at urination sites of animals and at old campfires.

Butterflies become very absorbed when feeding at these sites, especially when on dung or carrion, and will allow you to get very close. Sometimes you can approach so close that you can actually pick them up briefly by the wings.

Tiger swallowtails are one of the species that most commonly puddle. Mostly male butterflies visit puddles, where they get sodium and other nutrients.

The butterflies most commonly seen puddling are tiger swallowtails, blues, and sulphurs. Other species that puddle include other swallowtails, fritillaries, anglewings, hackberry butterflies, satyrs, and several skippers (including the European skipper), as well as the cabbage white, buckeye, American painted lady, viceroy, white admiral, western admiral, and American copper. Moths, which may need the same nutrients, often visit the same puddling sites at night.

Courting

One of an adult butterfly's main tasks is finding a mate. This is not always easy since butterflies are small and usually exist in low densities.

In general, male butterflies actively seek out females, and they do it in two ways — perching and patrolling. Perching males fly to areas where they are likely to encounter females, such as paths, streams, or ridges along which females tend to move. Here they perch on vegetation or prominent objects, such as a rock or fallen log. When they think they see a female, they dart out to investigate. Because butterflies cannot visually distinguish fine details from a distance, these

males often end up exploring the wrong species or even the wrong type of animal. Sometimes even you may be inspected.

If the inspected object is not his species, then the male just returns to his perch. If it is his species, but a male, then he may chase it for a short distance, or the two may fly vertically into the air for a few feet, after which the original male generally returns to his perch. If the perching male discovers a female of his species, then he pursues her and begins active courting. Common species that use the perching strategy include the black swallowtail, red admiral, comma, and mourning cloak.

The other strategy of mate-finding is patrolling — flying about in areas where females may be feeding or laying eggs and exploring all objects that may be mates. Again, once they discover a female of their species, males begin actively courting. Common species that patrol are whites, sulphurs, and the monarch.

Courtship in butterflies is easy to recognize. At first, the male flies either above or behind the female, often with a more fluttering and rapid wingbeat than usual. During this time he may release scents (pheromones) from his wings or

Most butterflies, like this zebra swallowtail, bask by spreading their wings and turning their back to the sun.

body that may cause the female, if she is receptive, to land on the ground or nearby vegetation. In a few species, courtship may also involve tactile or visual displays of the male, such as touching the female with antennae or legs, or making unusual wing movements.

Once this initial phase of courtship is complete, and it may take only seconds, the male and female will end up side by side. Then the male will curve the tip of his abdomen toward the female, she curves hers toward him, and they copulate. Copulation may take from ten minutes to several hours. During copulation the two may take flight while still joined at the tips of their abdomens. The male or the female may fly carrying the other; the carried butterfly hangs underneath. These flights are conspicuous.

An already mated female may continue to be approached by courting males. In these cases she may have to avoid their advances. This can be done chemically, through so-called antiaphrodisiacs, or through actions. One common such action is for the female to bend her abdomen up behind her in the air while perched — this makes it impossible for the male to make normal contact. Another is to spread her wings, thus preventing the male from getting near enough to mate. A third behavior, commonly seen in sulphurs but also in many other species, is for the female to spiral up in flight when approached. She and the male keep going higher and higher until the male gives up and drops to the ground. She then floats down more slowly. All of these avoidance mechanisms can be readily seen in the field, especially where there are high concentrations of butterflies.

Basking

Butterflies fly best when their body temperature is about 85–100°F. In order to fly well when air temperatures are cooler than this, they need to warm their bodies to this point. This is accomplished through basking — using the sun's heat to warm up.

There are several different ways that butterflies bask, all easy to see in the field. The most common is called dorsal basking, in which the butterfly opens its wings all the way out and orients them perpendicular to the sun's rays. Heat is absorbed by the body of the butterfly (which is often black) and by the area of the wings closest to the body. Early spring generations in some species have darker areas on these parts of the wings to help them warm up faster in cooler weather.

Another type of basking is called lateral basking, in which the wings are closed and the butterfly turns its side toward the sun. This is commonly seen in sulphurs and many satyrs. In these species it is the amount of dark area at the base of the outer hind wing that affects the rate of their warming.

Recent research has discovered another strategy, known as reflectance basking, in which the wings act as solar reflectors rather than absorbers; they are angled so that they reflect light down onto the butterfly's body. In this case, the lighter the color of the outermost portions of the wings, the better warming they produce, just the opposite of the situation with dorsal and lateral baskers. This behavior occurs in some whites.

A female zebra swallowtail laying her egg on a pawpaw leaf.

Most butterflies start basking in the morning. They can be found sitting on vegetation oriented toward the sun. On days when the temperature is below 80°F, even a large cloud passing in front of the sun will make butterflies land and start basking.

Egg Laying

After mating, a female's main job is laying eggs. An egg-laying female is generally easy to spot — she is often away from flowers, flying low over vegetation in a fluttery manner, and repeatedly touching down or landing on various plants.

Females can recognize certain families, genera, or species of plants through sensory cues. From a distance of several feet, they may use visual cues, such as the color or shape of leaves. As they get closer, they may pick up scents with their antennae. Once on the plant, they may touch it with their antennae or their proboscis, or taste it with their feet. You may see a female tap on the leaf with her front feet. This behavior, called drumming, scratches the leaf surface to release chemicals that she can then identify; it may also help the female evaluate the texture or health of the leaf. In some cases, females are known to avoid plants that already have butterfly eggs or caterpillars on them.

Once a female has found a suitable plant, she bends the tip of her abdomen down to deposit an egg on the top or bottom surface of the leaf. Following an egg-laying female is the best way to find butterfly eggs.

A few species of butterflies do not lay their eggs on specific plants but more generally broadcast them over a habitat. This is especially true of species whose caterpillars feed on grasses, such as wood nymphs and satyrs.

Most species lay their eggs singly, just one egg on each leaf. Only a few species lay eggs in clusters of 10 to 300 or more on the same leaf.

HOW TO REAR BUTTERFLIES

Finding Eggs, Caterpillars, and Pupae

Rearing the eggs, caterpillars, and pupae of butterflies in your home can be a lot of fun and one of the best ways to learn about butterfly lives. To do this you must first find the early stage of a butterfly. This can happen in several ways. It is highly unlikely that you will come across a butterfly egg by chance, for they are just too small. But it is a common experience to find a female butterfly in the process of laying eggs (see page 31). In this case, just watch which leaf she attaches the egg or eggs to and collect the sprig of the plant that contains it. Obviously, hatching eggs will give you caterpillars, but caterpillars are also sometimes found by chance or through careful looking on specific food plants.

If you are raising a caterpillar, you will end up with a pupa. You may also find a pupa, but this is unlikely, since they are well camouflaged and often formed away from the food plant.

Providing for Eggs and Caterpillars

Once you have the young stage of a butterfly, your next job is caring for it. This means re-creating the kinds of environmental conditions that it would encounter in the wild.

With eggs found on green leaves, take a sprig of the plant and put its stem in water to keep it healthy.

For raising caterpillars, a small empty aquarium or even just a large plastic box or large glass jar with a wide mouth makes a good container. The lid or cover of the container should have a few holes in it for air circulation. To have healthy caterpillars, keep two conditions in mind — humidity and temperature. Caterpillars breathe through lots of tiny holes in the sides of their bodies called spiracles. They can lose a lot of moisture through these holes and dry out; they can also drown by taking in too much moisture, such as when a container is left in the sun, making the humidity too high. Try to keep your caterpillar container humid — more than average humidity — but not wet. To increase humidity, you can place a moist paper towel in the bottom of the container.

Temperature is also important. Insects do not internally regulate their body temperature as we do, but are warmed or cooled by air temperature and from being in sun or shade. It is best to keep your insect container out of direct sun, since this may warm a closed container so much that it can harm the insect. At the same time, if the container is in a very cool location, the temperature may slow down the insect's development.

Your main task when raising a caterpillar is providing it with enough food. Give it the leaves of the plant on which you found either it or the egg from which it hatched. If you know the species of the caterpillar, you can look up what other plants it may accept in the chapter on that species in the second half of this book.

When the caterpillar is small it will eat very little, but as it grows larger you may have to keep it supplied with new leaves each day. One way to keep the leaves fresh is to cover a small vase of water with plastic wrap and poke the stems of the plant through it and into the water. Then place this into your container. This makes sure that if the caterpillar crawls down the plant stem it will not end up in the water. You can also just lay some damp paper towels in the bottom of the container and put leaves on them, but the leaves will not stay as fresh.

Tiger swallowtail feeding at loose-strife. Some swallowtails, such as the black swallowtail and spicebush swallowtail, are easy to raise when you find their eggs or caterpillars.

A container for raising caterpillars.

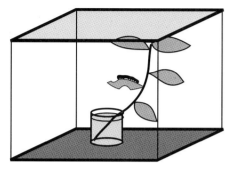

Caterpillar droppings will accumulate in the bottom of the container. These should be cleaned out regularly.

Remember that the caterpillar will become still when molting its skin. It is good to have a few extra twigs or sticks in the container for the caterpillar to crawl on when shedding or when looking for a place to pupate. Often, however, caterpillars will crawl up the sides of a container and pupate while hanging from the lid or cover.

Keeping Pupae and Adults

Keep pupae at an average outdoor temperature and humidity. When an adult emerges from a pupa, it hangs upside down while its wings expand and then harden. Without sufficient room, its wings may never expand fully, preventing it from flying. So be sure the pupa is in a large container and there is a way for the butterfly to crawl up on a branch or screen and hang upside down. It is difficult for it to climb up the sides of a glass jar.

Once the adult's wings have hardened, carry it outside in the container and place the opened container near flowers so that the butterfly can leave and feed.

Parasites and Wintering Stages

When raising caterpillars, you sometimes do not end up with an adult butterfly. Instead, you end up with a small fly or wasp. These are parasites that lay their eggs in the eggs, caterpillars, or pupae of butterflies. The eggs hatch and the young flies or wasps feed on the caterpillars (or pupae). Eventually, the caterpillar is killed and the adult parasite emerges.

When you collect immature stages in late summer or early fall it is important that you know the butterfly's overwintering stage. You may have an egg that does not hatch, a pupa that does not open, or a caterpillar that stops eating before it is full grown and starts wandering about. Each of these could be an overwintering stage.

In these cases, nothing more will happen until spring; however, it is important that you provide your butterfly with the right conditions for overwintering. Whether egg, caterpillar, or pupa, it needs to be placed outdoors and away from direct sun. If it is a caterpillar, you might provide it with some dry leaves and a little bark under which it can crawl. In spring you can bring it back inside, and it will resume its development.

The overwintering form of each species can be found under the species accounts in the last half of the book.

IDENTIFYING CATERPILLARS

Below are photographs of the later stages of our most common caterpillars, along with descriptions of characteristic traits of each butterfly family. These traits will help you identify species not shown to at least their family level. Pupae are less often found; nonetheless, a few examples are shown on page 21.

Only mature caterpillars are pictured here; younger stages of the same species can look quite different. For example, some swallowtail larvae look like bird droppings in their early stages, but have big eyespots when older.

Many caterpillars you will find are those of moths. Some of the more common are covered by numerous fine hairs, like the woolly bear. Very few of our butterfly caterpillars are woolly; most are smooth or have spines.

Fritillaries, Crescents, Anglewings, Tortoiseshells, Painted Ladies, Admirals, Longwings, Buckeye

Family: Brush-Footed Butterflies

Medium-sized caterpillars, numerous branched spines, evenly cylindrical, often crosswise stripes. Up to 1–2 in. long.

Gulf fritillary

Zebra

Great spangled fritillary

Baltimore

Question mark

Comma

Mourning cloak

Milbert's tortoiseshell

American painted lady

Painted lady

West Coast lady

Red admiral

Buckeye

White admiral

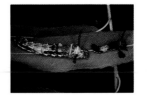
Viceroy

Red-spotted purple

Swallowtails
Family: Swallowtails
Generally smooth, front end often larger than hind end, hornlike projections extruded when disturbed, may have fake eyespots or vertical stripes. Up to 2¼ in. long.

Pipevine swallowtail

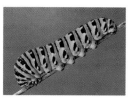

Black swallowtail

Anise swallowtail

Giant swallowtail

Tiger swallowtail

Spicebush swallowtail

Zebra swallowtail

Whites and Sulphurs
Family: Whites and Sulphurs
Thin, evenly cylindrical, generally green with longitudinal or horizontal stripes, smooth or with very short fine hairs. Often found on mustards and legumes. Most up to 1 in. long; cloudless sulphur up to 2 in. long.

Cabbage white

Checkered white

Falcate orange tip

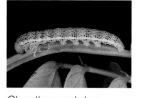

Dog face

Cloudless sulphur

Hairstreaks, Coppers, Blues
Family: Gossamer Wings
Short, broad, flattened, very different from other caterpillars, more sluglike, legs not obvious and head can be retracted, covered with very short hairs. Up to ½ in. long.

Banded hairstreak

Gray hairstreak

Monarch and Queen
Family: Milkweed butterflies
Smooth with numerous alternating light and dark crosswise bands; pair of antenna-like projections at each end (queen has a third pair near middle). Up to 2 in. long.

Monarch

Queen

Satyrs
Family: Satyrs

Hackberry Butterflies
Family: Hackberry Butterflies

Tapered at both ends, green, two taillike projections at hind end (hackberry butterflies have branched horns on head). Up to 1¼ in. long.

Eyed brown

Tawny emperor

Skippers
Family: Skippers

Large dark head, neck thinner than rest of body, often found feeding in leafy tent. Up to 1¼ in. long.

Silver-spotted skipper

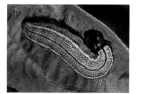

Long-tailed skipper

IDENTIFYING ADULT BUTTERFLIES

How Many Butterflies

There are about 17,000 species of butterflies in the world. In North America there are just about as many species of butterflies as there are of birds — around 700. To learn to identify them all is a formidable task. However, only a small fraction of these species are really common and likely to be seen by the average person. The 63 species in this book include the most widespread and common in gardens and backyards. If you learn these butterflies, you will be able to identify most of the species that you encounter.

How to Use This Identification Guide

When you see a butterfly, watch it closely for several minutes. See how it flies — is it rapid or slow, bobbing or sailing, high or low? Look at its size — is it large, medium, or small? Look at its wing shape — do the wings have rounded edges, irregular edges, pointed tips, or tails coming off the back? And look at its colors — do the wings have different upper and lower surfaces, do they have bands or spots, are they light or dark?

Once you have had a good look at it, flip through the next six pages of this book and find your butterfly. The species are grouped by family, and all are shown life size. Under the butterfly is the species' common name, its scientific name, and important clues that help distinguish this species from others that are like it.

There is also a page number, telling you where to find the chapter that offers a full description of the life and behavior of that species and its relatives. In that chapter, you will see another picture of that species as it looks in the wild.

Start by Knowing the Families

One of the best ways to start knowing the butterflies is to learn to recognize certain families of butterflies that are distinctive. Below is a list of the most easily identified families and some of their observable characteristics.

Swallowtails — Swallowtails are our largest butterflies, and most have long tails coming off their hind wings. Their flight is strong and may include glides. Many are black with striking yellow markings, or yellow with black stripes. They are seen often where there are lots of flowers.

Whites and Sulphurs — These are all medium-sized butterflies that are predominantly white or yellow. They fly in a continuous fluttering manner and are conspicuous along roadsides, in meadows, and in gardens.

Gossamer Wings — This group is easy to identify since it includes all of our smallest butterflies, such as the blues, coppers, hairstreaks, and metalmarks. The blues tend to be iridescent blue, coppers are often copper, hairstreaks often have hairlike tails on their hind wings, and metalmarks often have metallic spots on their wings.

Brush-Footed Butterflies — This is a large and varied group of medium-sized, generally dark-colored butterflies with such strong and rapid flight that they are hard to follow. There is no one field characteristic, besides their flight, that makes them easy to identify as a group.

Satyrs — These are medium-sized butterflies that are almost all brown, often with darker eyespots on their wings. They have a weak and bobbing flight and are often seen at woods edges or among grasses.

Skippers — Skippers are small butterflies whose flight is extremely rapid and erratic. They are mostly rich browns or orange-brown.

Spicebush Swallowtail — *Papilio troilus* Dark wings. Prominent single row of white spots on forewings; greenish-blue wash on hind wings. P. 44.

Black Swallowtail — *Papilio polyxenes* Dark with two rows of prominent yellowish spots along forewing edge. P. 44.

Tiger Swallowtail — *Papilio glaucus* Dark-form female. Note red spot on hind wings, and faint row of dots near forewing edge. P. 44.

Pipevine Swallowtail — *Battus philenor* Dark forewings. Iridescent blue hind wings with a few light markings. P. 44.

Anise Swallowtail — *Papilio zelicaon* Large yellow band through center of forewing. P. 44.

Tiger Swallowtail — *Papilio glaucus* Light form. Black and yellow tiger stripes. Differs from western tiger swallowtail by range. P. 44.

Giant Swallowtail — *Papilio cresphontes*
Yellow band crosses through center of forewing, tails
with yellow centers. P. 44.

Zebra Swallowtail — *Eurytides marcellus*
White with black stripes. Longest tails of any
swallowtail. P. 44.

Phoebus Parnassian — *Parnassius
phoebus* White wings with black and
red spots. P. 44.

Dog Face — *Colias cesonia*
Yellow with "dog face" outlined in
black border. P. 54.

Clouded Sulphur — *Colias philodice*
Yellow with dark border. (Female
shown; male with solid black border.)
P. 54.

Checkered White — *Pontia protodice* White with brown patches. P. 50.

Western White — *Pontia occidentalis* Similar to checkered white but
darker. Distinguished from it by range.
P. 50.

Alfalfa Sulphur — *Colias eurytheme*
Orange wings with black border. (Male
shown; female with light spots in dark
border). P. 54.

Cabbage White — *Pieris rapae*
White with dark tip to forewing. One
dark spot on male forewing, two dark
spots on female forewing. P. 50.

Falcate Orange Tip — *Anthocharis midea* Irregular forewing
edge. Male forewings orange
tipped. P. 50.

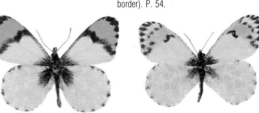

Sara Orange Tip — *Anthocharis sara*
White with orange tips to forewing. Female may be
yellow. Male, left; female, right. P. 50.

Cloudless Sulphur — *Phoebis sennae* Yellow without black markings. P. 54.

Mormon Metalmark — *Apodemia mormo* Dark wings spotted with white. P. 58.

Silvery Blue — *Glaucopsyche lygdamus* Male iridescent blue on upper surface. Female blue to brown with dark border. P. 62.

Spring Azure — *Celastrina argiolus* Upper surface iridescent blue; no tails. P. 62.

Snout — *Libytheana bachmanii* Mouthparts appear as a prominent snout. P. 64.

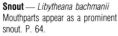

Dainty Sulphur — *Nathalis iole* Small. Yellow with black tip to forewing and dark along base of forewing. P. 54.

Purplish Copper — *Epidemia helloides* Male purplish with black spots (left). Female tawny with black spots (right). P. 58.

Eastern Tailed Blue — *Everes comyntas* Male iridescent blue on upper surface, with small tail on each hind wing (left). Female brown with tails (right). Differs from western tailed blue by range. P. 62.

Brown Elfin — *Incisalia augustinus* Small brown butterfly with a scalloped edge to the hind wing. P. 60.

Hackberry Butterfly — *Asterocampa celtis* Dark with brown or tan markings. One black eyespot on forewing. Hind wings triangular. P. 64.

American Copper — *Lycaena phlaeas* Bright orange forewings, dark hind wings with orange band. P. 58.

Gray Hairstreak — *Strymon melinus* Upper surface gray to brown, with red-orange spot at edge of each hind wing near a small tail. P. 60.

Banded Hairstreak — *Satyrium calanus* Dark gray on upper surface, gray to brown on undersurface. Small tails on hind wings with blue and orange spots underneath. P. 60.

Tawny Emperor — *Asterocampa clyton* Tawny forewings with yellow spots and dark wavy bands. Hind wings triangular. P. 64.

Gulf Fritillary — *Agraulis vanillae* Long wings, orange with black lines. Large silver spots on undersurface. P. 66.

Zebra — *Heliconius charitonius* Long black wings with slashes of yellow. P. 66.

Question Mark — *Polygonia interrogationis* Irregular edge to wings, with violet on margins. Short tails on hind wings. P. 68.

Comma — *Polygonia comma* Irregular edge to wings. Short, stubby tails. Forewings orange with dark blotches. P. 68.

Milbert's Tortoiseshell — *Nymphalis milberti* Bright yellow band just inside dark margin of wings. P. 68.

Mourning Cloak — *Nymphalis antiopa* Dark wings with broad yellow margins. P. 68.

Buckeye — *Junonia coenia* One large and one small eyespot on hind wings. P. 72.

Red Admiral — *Vanessa atalanta* Dark with red-orange stripes through center of forewings and along margins of hind wings. P. 72.

American Painted Lady — *Vanessa virginiensis* Yellowish bar on front edge of forewing, white spots at the tip. Undersurface has two large spots at margin of hind wing. Smaller than painted lady. P. 72.

Painted Lady — *Vanessa cardui* White bar on front edge of forewing, white spots at the tip. Undersurface has four spots at margin of hind wing. P. 72.

West Coast Lady — *Vanessa annabella* Similar to American painted lady, but all four spots on hind wing upper surfaces have blue centers. Bar on front edge of forewing orange. P. 72.

Great Spangled Fritillary — *Speyeria cybele* Orange with dark zigzag lines, dots, and chevrons. Hind wing undersurface has large silver spots and wide yellow band near border. P. 76.

Meadow Fritillary — *Boloria bellona* Small fritillary, rust-colored underneath. P. 76.

Pearl Crescent — *Phyciodes tharos* Orange with wide black border and complex markings on wings. Male, left; female, right. P. 78.

Baltimore — *Euphydryas phaeton* Black with white dots and red-orange spots along margin. P. 78.

Red-Spotted Purple — *Limenitis arthemis astyanax* Black butterfly with bluish iridescence near edge of hind wings and no tails. P. 80.

White Admiral — *Limenitis arthemis arthemis* Black butterfly with white bands on forewings and hind wings. Differs from western admiral by band width and range. P. 80.

Viceroy — *Limenitis archippus* Like monarch but smaller with an extra line of black across the hind wings. P. 80.

Western Admiral — *Limenitis weidemeyerii* Black butterfly with wide white bands along forewings and hind wings. Differs from white admiral by band width and range. P. 80.

Sister — *Adelpha bredowii* Dark with white band crossing both wings. Orange on forewings bordered by black. P. 80.

Lorquin's Admiral — *Limenitis lorquini* Dark with cream-colored bands crossing both wings. Orange tips not bordered by black, but extend to edge of wing. P. 80.

Northern Eyed Brown — *Satyrodes eurydice* Tan to brown wings with three to four eyespots at margins of both wings. P. 84.

Common Wood Nymph — *Cercyonis pegala* Light to dark brown with two dark eyespots on forewings, sometimes surrounded by a yellowish area. Two variations shown above. P. 84.

Ringlet — *Coenonympha tullia* Orange-brown to tan. Small and plain. Forewing sometimes has a small dark eyespot. P. 84.

Little Wood Satyr — *Megisto cymela* Gray-brown with two black eyespots neatly rimmed with yellow on forewing. Hind wing similar. P. 84.

Long-Tailed Skipper — *Urbanus proteus* Dark wings with long tails that have some greenish iridescence. P. 92.

European Skipper — *Thymelicus lineola* Tawny orange with fine dark border. P. 92.

Silver-Spotted Skipper — *Epargyreus clarus* Dark brown with faint, lighter rectangular spots on forewing. Hindwing undersurface has large irregular silver spot. P. 92.

Fiery Skipper — *Hylephila phyleus* Yellow-orange wings with irregularly edged dark border. Female, left; male, right. P. 92.

Queen — *Danaus gilippus* Deep red-brown with dark margins and white spots scattered about tips of forewings. Undersurface similar to monarch. P. 88.

Monarch — *Danaus plexippus* Orange with black border and black veins. P. 88.

THE BUTTERFLIES

Species Accounts

Once you have planted your butterfly gardens and have identified the butterflies that are attracted there to feed and lay their eggs, then you can enjoy learning more about their lives. Butterfly behavior is interesting, often amazing, as well as easy to observe. The following species accounts give you all kinds of information about your butterfly visitors. Below is a short explanation of how some of this information is presented.

Names — At the start of each chapter you will see the name of the family to which the group of butterflies belongs. Following that is a list of the species included in the chapter, with both their common and scientific names. We have based common names on the Xerces Society list. In cases where there is another long-standing common name, we have included it in parentheses.

There is disagreement on the scientific names of some butterflies. We have based our scientific names on those given in the checklist of the Lepidopterists' Society. We have included alternative scientific names, for easy reference to other books.

Charts — At the end of each chapter is a chart with important facts about each species. At the top of each chart is a rough approximation of the length of that group's life stages (egg, larva, pupa, adult) in summer, with days, weeks, and/or months indicated after each icon. For each species, the chart shows: habitat, main larval foods, main adult foods, flight period, number of broods (generations) per year, and stage in which they overwinter. Flight period refers to the months of the year when you can see adults flying about. As you can see from the charts, both flight period and number of broods vary from south to north, with shorter flight periods and fewer broods occurring in the North.

Families of Butterflies

In scientific classification, similar species are grouped into a genus, and like genera are grouped into a family. Knowing these relationships is helpful in identification and in understanding behavior and life histories. Below is a summary list of the families of common butterflies and their location in the book.

Butterfly Families

SWALLOWTAILS

Pipevine Swallowtail — *Battus philenor*
Zebra Swallowtail — *Eurytides marcellus*
Anise Swallowtail — *Papilio zelicaon*
Black Swallowtail — *Papilio polyxenes*
Giant Swallowtail — *Papilio (or Heraclides) cresphontes*
Spicebush Swallowtail — *Papilio (or Pterourus) troilus*

Tiger Swallowtail — *Papilio (or Pterourus) glaucus*
Western Tiger Swallowtail — *Papilio (or Pterourus) rutulus*
Phoebus Parnassian (Small Apollo) — *Parnassius phoebus*

Probably more than any other group, the swallowtails epitomize the beauty, vibrant color, and grace of butterflies. Their large size makes them conspicuous visitors to any garden, and their gorgeous colors make them prized additions to any

The tiger swallowtail (shown here) and western tiger swallowtail look similar and are best distinguished by geographic distribution.

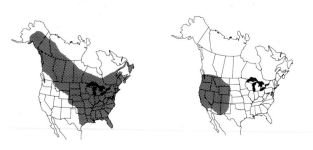

Tiger Swallowtail   Western Tiger Swallowtail

scene. Swallowtails are in the swallowtail family (Papilionidae), named for the taillike projections on their hind wings, which resemble the tails of swallows.

The family is divided into two subfamilies: the swallowtails (Papilioninae) and the parnassians (Parnassiinae). The parnassians, in contrast to the swallowtail subfamily, are medium-sized butterflies without tails and are mostly white with red and black spots and live in northern and mountain areas. Members of the swallowtail subfamily live mostly in tropical and southern regions.

Swallowtails fly with slow wingbeats as they move from flower to flower, but when disturbed they fly quickly and strongly away, often up to the tops of trees. While feeding they often continue to open and close their wings, possibly for balance.

How to Attract

Adults: Adult swallowtails prefer to feed from taller flowers. Being large, they have long mouthparts and can feed from longer-tubed flowers than most other butterflies. Most prefer to have some trees near where they feed.

Larvae: There are several plants you might plant in your yard to attract certain species of swallowtails: spicebush and sassafras for spicebush swallowtails; parsley and carrots for black swallowtails; pipevines for pipevine swallowtails; and pawpaw for zebra swallowtails. Black cherry and aspen can attract female tiger swallowtails for egg laying, especially if good nectar plants are nearby.

Other: Male swallowtails love to visit puddles. Try maintaining a puddle or moist sandy area for them to visit for the added nutrients they need.

Spicebush swallowtails can be told from other swallowtails by their single row of prominent white dots inside the margin of their forewings.

Spicebush Swallowtail

Look-alikes

If you have trouble telling certain swallowtails apart, you are not alone. Several swallowtails have evolved to look similar for the purpose of protection. Here is how it all works.

Caterpillars of the pipevine swallowtail feed on pipevines (*Aristolochia* spp.), which contain noxious chemicals called aristolochic acids. These chemicals are stored in their bodies, making the caterpillars and adults distasteful to birds, who learn to recognize these butterflies and then avoid eating them in the future.

Several other species of butterflies have evolved to look like the pipevine swallowtail and thus fool some birds into thinking that they are also distasteful. Mimics include the black swallowtail, spicebush swallowtail, and some female tiger swallowtails, as well as the red-spotted purple, which is one of the admirals.

Female tiger swallowtails can develop into one of two color forms — the familiar tigerlike form, with yellow and black stripes, and a darker form, mostly black with blue on the hind wings. The dark form is actually a mimic of the pipevine swallowtail. Dark-form females generally produce

This resting spicebush swallowtail shows the underwing pattern, which mimics that of the pipevine swallowtail.

Giant swallowtails can be recognized by the large yellow bands through their forewings. Also note the yellow centers to their tails.

Giant Swallowtail

dark-form daughters, and yellow females produce yellow daughters. In areas where there are more pipevine swallowtails, there is also a greater proportion of dark-form to light-form female tiger swallowtails.

Dropping Out of Sight

Many birds eat caterpillars, and because of this, caterpillars have evolved several effective defenses. The small, young caterpillars of black, giant, anise, spicebush, and tiger swallowtails all look very much like bird droppings. They are dark with an irregular white marking across their back. This is not by chance and is a highly practical way to avoid being eaten by birds.

As the caterpillars grow larger, they can no longer effectively mimic the small bird droppings, and they become green, which camouflages them against the leaves on which they are feeding. Tiger and spicebush swallowtails take this two steps further — they both rest and feed in leaves that they have curled over themselves with silk, and both have large fake eyespots near their heads that make them look like small snakes, just in case they are discovered. They can even rear up in a threatening manner.

In addition, all swallowtail caterpillars have a forked gland, called the osmeterium, that can be everted from the back just behind the head. This releases a bad smell that repels smaller predators. You can get this response with a gentle squeeze of your thumb and forefinger along the front portion of the caterpillar. The osmeterium will appear like an orange forked tongue. You may be able to smell it; several species reek of rancid butter.

Hilltopping

Sometimes you may encounter several black or anise swallowtails flying over a hilltop or along a ridge. This is called hilltopping. These butterflies all tend to fly up hills, thereby increasing their density on hill- and ridgetops so that males and females can find each other more easily. Black swallowtail males in the East and anise swallowtail males in the West are persistent patrollers, remaining in such areas for hours each day and several days in a row.

If another male intrudes on the territory of a hilltopping swallowtail, the two engage in rapid chases and ascending flights. If the butterfly that flies by is a female swallowtail, then the male begins courting her by repeatedly flying up in

The zebra swallowtail is one of the most striking. Its greenish white background with black stripes is distinctive. It also has the longest tails of any of our common swallowtails.

Zebra Swallowtail

front of her. Mating follows if the female is receptive. Male swallowtails that control the most preferred sites encounter and chase more intruding males, but they also encounter and mate with more females.

Choosing Leaves

Female swallowtails use various means to find the right plants on which to lay their eggs. While flying, female black swallowtails land more often on carrot plants (their food plant) when they smell the leaves. After landing, they taste the leaves through a characteristic drumming behavior — tapping their forelegs alternately to expose the chemicals on the leaf's surface.

Pipevine swallowtails choose plants for egg laying by sight as well as taste. In Texas, two of their food plants grow together, one with narrow leaves (*Aristolochia serpentaria*) and one with broader leaves (*A. reticulata*). Individual females learn, through their first encounter with one of the two, to search for that leaf shape. They continue preferring leaves of that shape unless they happen to land on a leaf of the other shape; they then may switch search modes or stay with the same leaf shape.

The phoebus parnassian is in a subfamily different from that of the rest of the swallowtails in this chapter. Notice that it has no tails.

Phoebus Parnassian

The pipevine swallowtail is distinctive in that it has no interior markings on its dark forewings.

Pipevine Swallowtail

New Cuisine

Centuries ago in California, anise swallowtails could emerge and fly only in spring because their native food plants, various members of the carrot family, died back during the hot California summers. Then, in the 1700s, Spaniards introduced sweet fennel (*Foeniculum vulgare*) — another carrot relative from Europe — to California, and it spread rapidly. Sweet fennel keeps growing in cultivated and urbanized areas throughout the summer; it is chemically similar to the native food plants, so anise swallowtails lay their eggs on it. Anise swallowtails have followed the spread of sweet fennel. They now produce several generations each year and are becoming more abundant.

The Spaniards also introduced orange trees to California, with orange groves appearing in the 1840s. By 1918, anise swallowtails had begun to lay their eggs on the leaves of orange trees as well. Though the orange tree is a member of a different plant family, its leaves are chemically similar to fennel. The chemicals they have in common are known as essential oils, and they stimulate the caterpillars to feed as well as females to lay eggs.

The black swallowtail generally has two distinct rows of lighter dots inside the edge of the forewings.

Black Swallowtail

The anise swallowtail has a broad yellow band through the center of the forewings.

Anise Swallowtail

Chastity Belts

During mating, a male parnassian secretes a waxy material on the female's abdomen that hardens into a specific shape for each different species of parnassian. In the phoebus parnassian this struc-ture — called the sphragis — is brown with a projecting ridge. You can see it very clearly on any mated female you find. The sphragis serves as a chastity belt by blocking access to the female's genitalia. A female can continue to lay eggs, for she has another opening where eggs are produced.

Swallowtails

4–10 days   3–4 weeks   10–20 days   6–14 days

Common Name	Habitat	Larval Food	Adult Food	Flight Period (Broods)	Winter Stage
Pipevine swallowtail	Woods, open brush	Pipevines	Nectar, puddling	South: Feb–Nov (4) North: Apr–Sep (2)	Pupa
Zebra swallowtail	Open, moist woods	Pawpaw	Nectar, puddling	South: Feb–Dec (4) North: May–Aug (1)	Pupa
Anise swallowtail	Lowlands, mountains	Sweet fennel, biscuit root, citrus trees	Nectar, puddling	South: Mar–Nov (3) North: May–Jul (1)	Pupa
Black swallowtail	Open areas	Wild carrot, dill, parsley, parsnip	Nectar, puddling	South: Mar–Nov (3) North: May–Sep (2)	Pupa
Giant swallowtail	Woods, brush, citrus groves	Prickly ash, hop tree, citrus trees	Nectar, dung, puddling	South: All year (2–3) North: May–Sep (2)	Pupa
Spicebush swallowtail	Woods, brush	Sassafras, spicebush	Nectar, puddling	South: Apr–Oct (3) North: May–Sep (2)	Pupa
Tiger swallowtail	Moist wooded areas	South: black cherry, tulip tree, sweet bay; North: aspens	Nectar, puddling	South: Mar–Nov (3) North: May–Jul (1)	Pupa
Western tiger swallowtail	Wooded areas, suburbs	Aspens, poplars, willows, alders, ashes	Nectar, puddling	South: Mar–Sep (3) North: Jun–Jul (1)	Pupa
Phoebus parnassian	Mountain meadows	Stonecrops	Nectar	South: May–Jun (1) North: Jul–Aug (1)	Egg or larva

WHITES

Falcate Orange Tip — *Anthocharis midea*
Sara Orange Tip — *Anthocharis sara*
Cabbage White — *Pieris rapae*
Checkered White (Common White) — *Pontia protodice*
Western White — *Pontia occidentalis*

At almost any given time, whites are among the butterflies you will be most likely to see. This is because they are abundant and attracted to wild and cultivated plants in gardens, fields, and road-sides. They are also among the first to appear in spring.

Whites belong to the family of whites and sulphurs (Pieridae). They are medium-sized butterflies that live up to their name — most are white, with a few black or orange markings. The flight of whites is straight and constantly fluttering, with little gliding. Most whites choose mustards (family Cruciferae) as food plants.

The bright colors — white, yellow, and orange — of whites and sulphurs are unique to these butterflies. These pigments come from the uric acid wastes produced from metabolizing protein. Whites are conspicuous to predators but not eaten because they may taste bad.

Flower Choice

If you watch an individual butterfly for a while, you will see that it tends to visit the same types of flowers for a long period of time. Among cabbage whites, individuals are able to learn how to get nectar from one type of flower; they then become

This cabbage white is getting nectar from a favorite source, loosestrife. It is recognized by being all white except for a dark tip to the forewings and one or two dark spots.

Cabbage White

How to Attract

Adults: Whites are not hard to attract. They particularly love wide-open areas. In spring they visit dandelions and winter cress; in summer, red clover and loosestrife are favorites; in fall, asters.

Larvae: Female whites lay their eggs on members of the mustard family, which includes cultivated vegetables such as cabbage and broccoli, and wildflowers such as winter cress, mustards, and peppergrass.

Other: You might try setting aside a few vegetable plants just for whites to lay their eggs on, and be sure not to spray them. Also, any sunny area of earth scraped bare will sprout up with peppergrass and some mustards and be a good place for these butterflies.

Western White   Checkered White

This western white is very similar to the checkered white except that its dark markings are generally black, whereas those of the checkered white are brownish.

more efficient at it. However, they have limited memory capacity, so if they then learn to feed from a second type of flower, they become less efficient at feeding from the first type. Therefore, a butterfly can gather nectar more rapidly by continuing to feed from flowers of the same type.

If you watch long enough, you may see the same individual switch to a new type of flower. This generally occurs when the amount of nectar in its previous flower type declines or when the butterfly has been disturbed and flies to a new location.

The flowers that are most attractive to butterflies are those with abundant nectar. But female cabbage whites are even more attracted if the nectar also contains amino acids, which are the building blocks of the proteins needed for egg production.

Where to Lay Eggs

How do female whites find plants in the mustard family? The answer may be chemicals. Plants in the mustard family all contain certain compounds known as mustard oils. Tests have shown that simply soaking a piece of paper with sinigrin, one of these compounds, is enough to make female cabbage whites lay their eggs on it.

But chemistry is not the complete story. When paper disks have the same chemicals in them, cabbage whites choose yellow, green, light blue, and white disks over purple, red, or dark disks. The butterflies can also learn to associate certain chemicals with certain colors. So to distinguish the correct food plants in the field, a female butterfly uses sight, smell, and taste. Of these, taste is the most important.

The falcate orange tip is similar to the sara orange tip except that the tips of its forewings are pointed.

Falcate Orange Tip

Seeing Red

Even when you look carefully, it is difficult to find most butterfly eggs, because they are pale colored and camouflaged. You can, however, find the eggs of many whites and sulphurs. When laid, the eggs of whites are yellow to pale green, but within a few hours the eggs of some species change to a conspicuous (against the paler green color of the food plant) red or orange. This odd occurrence requires some explanation.

Food plants for whites are often small, and a single caterpillar can eat most of the plant during its development. Because of this, when a female finds a red egg on her food plant, she tends not to lay there and instead flies off to find another plant. Some butterflies recognize and respond to red eggs produced by other species of butterflies, in addition to responding to red eggs of their own species.

A group of western mustard plants, called jewel flowers (*Streptanthus* spp.), have orange-red growths along their leaf margins that resemble the eggs of whites. Whites perceive these growths to be red eggs laid by other butterflies and generally avoid laying eggs on the plants. This egg mimicry is the reason jewel flowers are fed upon by caterpillars less than other mustards.

Staying Warm

Whites bask in the sun's rays in a posture unique to their group. In what is called reflectance basking, they orient their wings toward the sun at an angle so that solar energy is reflected off their white wings and onto their darker bodies. The darker the markings on their wings, the more open they hold them.

How dark markings affect body temperature depends on what part of the wings is dark. Darkening at the base of the wings, near the body, increases the rate of body warming, while darkening near the outer edges of the wings actually reduces the reflectivity of the wings and so keeps the body cooler.

Avoiding Advances

An adult female white spends most of her time looking for places to lay her eggs. On the other hand, a male white's main job is to find females and mate with them. Since the advances of males can take up important time that the female needs to lay eggs, females have evolved several ways to avoid this disturbance. In dense populations of checkered whites, females move away to new habitats, leaving males behind in areas of concentration. In other cases, a female may spread her wings and lift her abdomen up, both of which make it impossible for the male to mate with her.

Males also may attempt to mate with a female immediately after she has emerged from her pupal case. This can be a problem, because if she mates before her wings have expanded and dried, the wings may not expand properly, making it harder for her to fly. A cabbage white female prevents mating during wing drying by adopting the posture described above, of wings open and abdomen up.

The sara orange tip is recognized by its white wings with rounded orange tips on the forewings.

Sara Orange Tip

Whites

| | 4–7 days | | 2–4 weeks | | 8–14 days | | 6–10 days |

Common Name	Habitat	Larval Food	Adult Food	Flight Period (Broods)	Winter Stage
Falcate orange tip	Open woodlands	Mustards	Nectar	South: Mar–May (1) North: Apr–Jun (1)	Pupa
Sara orange tip	Meadows, canyons	Mustards	Nectar	East: Mar–Jul (1) West: Feb–Jun (2)	Pupa
Cabbage white	All open areas	Mustards, especially cabbage, broccoli	Nectar, rarely puddling	South: All year (3 +) North: Apr–Oct (2)	Pupa
Checkered white	Meadows, fields	Mustards	Nectar	South: Mar–Sep (3 +) North: May–Oct (3)	Pupa
Western white	Mountain meadows	Mustards	Nectar	Low: May–Sep (2–3) High: Jul–Aug (1)	Pupa

SULPHURS

Alfalfa Sulphur (Orange Sulphur) — *Colias eurytheme*
Clouded Sulphur (Common Sulphur) — *Colias philodice*

Dog Face — *Colias (or Zerene) cesonia*
Dainty Sulphur — *Nathalis iole*
Cloudless Sulphur — *Phoebis sennae*

Sulphurs are yellow, medium-sized butterflies commonly seen in cultivated and abandoned fields, where they mostly choose members of the pea family (Leguminosae) as food plants. They belong to the family of whites and sulphurs (Pieridae).

Sulphurs fly steadily, with very little gliding; smaller species fly close to vegetation and larger ones several feet higher. Some sulphurs keep flying late into the fall. They all bask by closing their wings and turning sideways to the sun.

Spiral Flights

Have you ever seen two or more yellow butterflies spiraling up in the air together? This is actually the rejection of a courting male by a female.

Male sulphurs patrol over areas of flowers and larval food plants looking for mates. When a male finds a female, he flutters above her, and if she is receptive, she perches. The male then continues to flutter above her, touching her lightly with his legs or wings and at the same time releasing a chemical that further stimulates her. She flutters in response and then curves her abdomen down. He lands, they mate, and he may fly away with

On the underwing, the clouded sulphur has a silvery spot with two circles of red around it.

Clouded Sulphur

How to Attract

Adults: Adult sulphurs are easy to attract to any open area with a variety of flowers. Wildflowers such as dandelions and clover are often enough, but they are also attracted to a wide variety of garden flowers. Try to have late-blooming flowers, for sulphurs can remain active well into fall.

Larvae: A vegetable garden is a good place to attract sulphurs, for they lay eggs on members of the pea family, such as beans. Marigolds, which may be planted around vegetable gardens to keep away pests, attract dainty sulphurs, as do many other composites.

Other: Sulphurs love to visit puddles, where there are concentrated salts and other nutrients. Keep a sandy or earthen area moist, and you may attract them to it.

The alfalfa sulphur is recognized by the orange on the wings; this one is identified as a female by the yellow dots in the black border of the forewings.

Alfalfa Sulphur

her hanging beneath. Mating may continue for up to an hour.

If the female has already mated, however, she is likely to reject the courting male. If perched, she may spread her wings and curve her abdomen up, making it impossible for him to mate with her. If flying, she may start to spiral upward as he follows. Watch the butterflies rise and you will see that he soon gives up and drops quickly to the ground, at which point she drifts down more slowly to continue flying by herself.

The Ultraviolet Sex

To us, male alfalfa and clouded sulphurs look similar, but to a female sulphur they are easy to tell apart. Ultraviolet light, which we cannot see, is visible to butterflies. Male alfalfa sulphurs reflect much more ultraviolet light than male clouded sulphurs. When males of both species approach a female, the differing amounts of ultraviolet reflection help the female choose an individual of the right species for mating.

Newly emerged females may be too weak to

reject suitors and thus may mate with males of the wrong species. Hybrids do occur regularly and are in color midway between the two species, with just a little orange appearing on the wings. Hybrid males do not reflect ultraviolet light, though, and so to females they look like clouded sulphurs.

Since the 1800s, the distribution and abundance of alfalfa and clouded sulphurs has increased dramatically. The widespread planting of alfalfa and clover fields has enabled both species to expand their ranges. Increased contact between the two species has led to more hybrids.

Females Come in Two Colors

Sometimes a spiral flight will seem to be between two species — one white and one yellow. Actually, female sulphurs, especially clouded, alfalfa, and cloudless sulphurs, can be yellow or white. Thus, in spiral flights between two colors of sulphurs, the female is the white one.

A white female is produced when some of the nitrogen resources from the caterpillar are not used to produce yellow pigments for the adult

The cloudless sulphur is all yellow with no black border on the upper wing surface of the male.

Cloudless Sulphur

Summer Travelers

Alfalfa and clouded sulphurs are distributed widely and overwinter throughout their range. Dog face, dainty, and cloudless sulphurs successfully overwinter only in the South. Even so, they are regularly seen every year many hundreds of miles to the north. This is because some migrate north each summer. The dainty sulphur populates the majority of its range through migration from southern population centers. These species take many weeks to fly north, so they are not seen in these areas until mid- to late summer, and not in all years.

Dark and Warm

As noted, all sulphurs bask with their wings closed and turned sideways to the sun. Sulphurs that live in northern areas or at high elevations are darker on the underwings. This is because more solar

The dainty sulphur is one of the smaller sulphurs. It has a dark area along the trailing edge of the forewing.

Dainty Sulphur

wings; they are reserved for future use of the adult in body maintenance and reproduction.

Male sulphurs are more attracted to yellow females, with which they mate more frequently. But white females develop faster, and their eggs mature faster, thanks to their stored resources.

There are proportionately more white females in colder climates — up to about 50 percent more in northeastern states — for with their additional resources they survive the cold better than yellow females. The balance tilts back in favor of yellow females in warmer areas, because males prefer them as mates.

The very distinctive pattern in the black border of the forewings inspired the dog face butterfly's name.

Dog Face

radiation is absorbed by darker surfaces, and as the underside of the hind wings warms up, so does the body itself. Furlike scales on the body retard heat loss.

In warmer climates, dark butterflies may become too hot, so at low elevations and farther south, sulphurs are lighter in color on the underwings. When the temperature is high, the butterflies minimize solar warming by perching with their folded wings pointed toward the sun.

Changes in the darkness of the wings take place seasonally as well. Sulphurs that emerge in spring are darker on the underwings than those that emerge in the heat of mid- to late summer.

Sulphurs

	3–7 days		2–4 weeks		7–14 days		6–10 days

Common Name	Habitat	Larval Food	Adult Food	Flight Period (Broods)	Winter Stage
Alfalfa sulphur	Open fields	Alfalfa, vetches, clovers	Nectar, puddling	South: Mar–Nov (5) North: May–Nov (3)	Larva or pupa
Clouded sulphur	Open fields	Clovers, alfalfa	Nectar, puddling	South: Mar–Nov (5) North: May–Nov (3)	Larva or pupa
Dog face	Open fields	Indigo bush, prairie clover	Nectar, puddling	South: All year (3) North: Jun–Oct (1–2)	Adult
Dainty sulphur	Open areas	Marigolds, sneezeweed	Nectar	South: All year (5) North: May–Oct (1)	Adult
Cloudless sulphur	Open areas	Sennas	Nectar, puddling	South: All year (3) North: Jun–Oct (1)	Adult

COPPERS AND METALMARKS

Mormon Metalmark — *Apodemia mormo*
Purplish Copper — *Epidemia* (or *Lycaena*) *helloides*

American Copper (Small Copper) — *Lycaena phlaeas*

Coppers and metalmarks are in the family of gossamer wings (Lycaenidae). This is a family of small butterflies that also includes blues and hairstreaks. The coppers and metalmarks are all small and frail in appearance and have sluglike caterpillars that are rarely seen because they are short and greenish.

As their name suggests, most coppers are iridescent orange or red, with various dark markings; a few are drab, though, and one is actually blue. Most coppers lay their eggs on plants in the buckwheat family (Polygonaceae), especially dock and sorrel (*Rumex* spp.). When flying, coppers are faster than blues but not as quick or erratic as hairstreaks.

Metalmarks are mostly tropical. They usually have metallic-looking flecks on their drab wings, but some, like the Mormon metalmark, are instead boldly checkered with white spots. They perch with their wings fully open and often pressed against their landing spot, such as under a leaf. Their flight is fast and erratic.

Copper Facts

The purplish copper is the most widespread copper in North America; it lives primarily in the West, where there are more species of coppers, and is the most abundant copper in California.

Eastern populations of the American copper are very similar to European "small coppers" and may have descended from butterflies accidentally introduced from Europe hundreds of years ago. American coppers in the East live along roadsides and in similar open habitats, while the same species in the West is found in mountainous regions. These butterflies form small populations in isolated sites.

Most coppers have one brood per year and overwinter in the egg stage. The American copper and

The Mormon metalmark is dark and covered with white spots.

Mormon Metalmark

How to Attract

Adults: Coppers and metalmarks take nectar from a wide variety of short-tubed flowers such as white clover, yarrow, and butterfly weed.

Larvae: Two common weeds attract both coppers for egg laying — sheep sorrel and curled dock (*Rumex* spp.). You may find these in any disturbed area or even as weeds in your garden. Leave them there and you may raise some butterflies.

In the American copper, the bright orange forewings contrast with the darker hind wings.

American Copper

The male purplish copper is dark with black spots on the wings and a wavy orange band at the outer edge of the hind wings.

Purplish Copper

purplish copper differ from this in that both can have 2 to 3 broods per year and overwinter in the larval stage.

Colorful Variations

The environmental conditions prevailing during the immature stages of American coppers can affect the appearance of the adults. For example, when the caterpillar is developing, the short days and cool temperatures of fall and winter result in the "spring form" of the adult butterfly, which is a lighter red. The long days and warm temperatures of summer lead to the dark "summer form" of the adult. This is why American copper adults are darker in summer and fall than in spring. The environment has the greatest effect during the larval stage, but chilling of the pupae in winter also affects the adult form.

There can also be variations in the appearance of adults resulting from their living in different habitats. For example, the wing color of Mormon metalmarks is darker in cooler, damper habitats and lighter in warmer, drier habitats.

Coppers and Metalmarks

| Coppers: | 5–7 days | 4 weeks | 10–20 days | 4–10 days |
| Metalmarks: | 10 days | 10 weeks | 10–20 days | 6–20 days? |

Common Name	Habitat	Larval Food	Adult Food	Flight Period (Broods)	Winter Stage
Mormon metalmark	Dry slopes, prairies	Wild buckwheat	Nectar	South: Mar–Oct (2+) North: Jul–Sep (1)	Larva
Purplish copper	Old fields, moist sites	Docks, knotweeds	Nectar	South: Apr–Oct (2+) North: Jul–Aug (1)	Larva
American copper	Fields, mountains, roadsides	Sorrels, docks	Nectar	East: Apr–Oct (2–4) West: Jun–Sep (1)	Larva

HAIRSTREAKS

Brown Elfin — *Incisalia augustinus*
Banded Hairstreak — *Satyrium calanus*
Gray Hairstreak (Common Hairstreak) — *Strymon melinus*

Hairstreaks are small, quick butterflies named for the hairlike tails on their hind wings and the thin, dark streaks on the undersurface of their wings. They belong to the family of gossamer wings (Lycaenidae) along with blues, coppers, and metalmarks. They are usually brown or gray with distinct markings. Elfins are brown hairstreaks without tails.

Hairstreaks are hard to find because of their size and because they often blend in with their background. They are best seen in the spring, perched on leaves or twigs along woods edges, from which they dart out in erratic flight. When perched they bask sideways in the sun.

The brown elfin is brown with darker brown near the body.

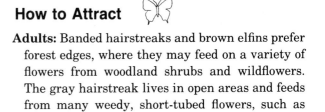

Brown Elfin

A Heady Deception

Hairstreaks have evolved so that the rear of their hind wings looks like their head. Most species have a conspicuous orange or red spot near the back edge of their hind wings and at the base of their thin tails. When the butterfly has its wings closed, the spots look like eyes, and the thin tails look like antennae. Often, the tails are white-tipped and more conspicuous than the real antennae. In addition, the portion of the wing with the eyespot may bend outward a little, thereby giving the appearance of a three-dimensional head. To add to the deception, many hairstreaks perch head down, which orients the false head upward.

Hairstreaks also shuffle their closed hind wings back and forth, making the tails move like antennae. Any predator that attacked a hairstreak might focus on the movement of the apparent head, grabbing the back of the wings rather than the real head, thus giving the butterfly a chance to escape. The wings on hairstreaks tear more easily near the eyespot than elsewhere, and hairstreaks observed in the field have been, in fact, more frequently attacked at the false head.

How to Attract

Adults: Banded hairstreaks and brown elfins prefer forest edges, where they may feed on a variety of flowers from woodland shrubs and wildflowers. The gray hairstreak lives in open areas and feeds from many weedy, short-tubed flowers, such as mustards, mints, and milkweeds.

Larvae: The banded hairstreak prefers oaks for egg laying, whereas the brown elfin chooses blueberries and relatives in open woods or boggy areas. The gray hairstreak is not very picky and will lay eggs on more species of plants than most of our other common butterflies.

On the underside of this gray hairstreak you can see the eyespots and tails that look like a head.

Gray Hairstreak

A lovely banded hairstreak feeding from an early flower of milkweed.

Banded Hairstreak

Courting Strategies

The density of the butterfly population can affect the strategy chosen by a male hairstreak to find a female. A study of gray hairstreaks in Arizona showed that males use two different tactics. In general, female gray hairstreaks emerge, feed, and lay eggs in such widely scattered locations that males are unlikely to find them simply by flying in random directions.

Females tend to disperse along ridges, so their density is higher in these locations. When populations are low, males choose perches on trees lo-

cated along these ridges and defend their perching spots against other males. Sometimes they defend the same tree for several days. When a female flies by, they dart out to meet her and start courting. They may also dart out to inspect other small butterflies, to see if they are female gray hairstreaks.

When population densities are higher, the energy needed to defend a territory against so many other males becomes too great. The male then abandons his territory and begins to fly from tree to tree along the ridges, increasing his chances of finding females.

Hairstreaks

 4–6 days   3–4 weeks   10–20 days   4–10 days

Common Name	Habitat	Larval Food	Adult Food	Flight Period (Broods)	Winter Stage
Brown elfin	Pine-oak forests, bogs	Blueberries, bearberry, and others	Nectar	South: Mar–Apr (1) North: May–Jun (1)	Pupa
Banded hairstreak	Oak woodland and edges	Oaks, hickories, butternut	Nectar	South: Apr–Jun (1) North: Jul–Aug (1)	Egg
Gray hairstreak	Weedy disturbed sites	Many plants, esp. legumes and mallows	Nectar	South: Feb–Oct (3+) North: May–Oct (2)	Pupa

BLUES

Spring Azure — *Celastrina argiolus*
Eastern Tailed Blue — *Everes comyntas*

Western Tailed Blue — *Everes amyntula*
Silvery Blue — *Glaucopsyche lygdamus*

Blues are little sparkling gems of the butterfly world. As long as the sun is out, they flutter about slowly and steadily over meadows filled with lupine and vetch, some of their favorite food plants. They belong to the family of gossamer wings (Lycaenidae), along with coppers, metalmarks, and hairstreaks.

Male blues are iridescent blue on the upper wing surfaces, sometimes with additional orange marks. Female blues are less brightly colored, being mostly brownish. Species are most readily distinguished by the different patterns on the undersides of their wings.

Blues are some of the smallest butterflies. In fact, one species, the pygmy blue of the American Southwest, is about the smallest butterfly in the world — less than half an inch across when the wings are fully spread.

Spring azures are beautiful early spring butterflies.

Spring Azure

Most blues are very restricted in their movements, and local populations periodically go extinct. Habitat change and late snowstorms that damage their food plants can lead to the loss of colonies. In California, the Xerces blue is now extinct because of urbanization, and the Karner blue in New York is now endangered for the same reason.

Ants for Friends

Many blues form mutualistic associations with ants. Caterpillars of blues secrete from their abdomens a sweet "honeydew," rich in sugars and protein, to which ants are attracted for feeding. They also have glands all over their skin that secrete components of protein — amino acids — that attract ants. The ants protect their source of food by repelling insect predators and parasites that would otherwise attack the caterpillars. In silvery blues, four to twelve times more caterpillars survive in the presence of ants.

The ants in turn benefit significantly from the nutrition provided by the caterpillar secretions, especially because they contain protein. To stimulate the flow of these secretions, ants brush their legs or antennae against the caterpillar's body. To satisfy their ants with protein, caterpillars of blues must feed on protein-rich plant parts, particularly flowers and seed pods.

How to Attract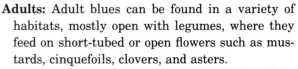

Adults: Adult blues can be found in a variety of habitats, mostly open with legumes, where they feed on short-tubed or open flowers such as mustards, cinquefoils, clovers, and asters.

Larvae: Many blues feed on clover, even the white clover of your lawn. Let some clover or vetch grow in an area for them.

With its wings folded up, this silvery blue blends in with the leaves.

Silvery Blue

The eastern tailed blue (shown here) is very similar to the western tailed blue. They are best told apart by their ranges, though they overlap in a few places.

Western Tailed Blue

Eastern Tailed Blue

Eggs and Seeds

Blues lay their eggs on flower buds of their legume hosts, and, once hatched, the caterpillars feed on the developing seeds in each flower. Silvery blues may consume more than half the seeds produced by a plant, enough to reduce significantly the number of host legumes that grow in an area where the butterflies live.

The butterflies lay their eggs only on immature flower buds; thus, the food plants can escape some caterpillar feeding damage by flowering early in the growing season. Early development, however, increases the likelihood of frost damage, so flowering does not take place too early, and the butterflies still find plenty of buds on which to lay their eggs.

Blues

3–6 days   2–3 weeks   8–12 days   4–10 days

Common Name	Habitat	Larval Food	Adult Food	Flight Period (Broods)	Winter Stage
Spring azure	Fields, forests	Dogwood, wild cherry, meadowsweet	Nectar, puddling	South: Feb–Nov (3) North: Apr–Sep (1)	Pupa
Eastern tailed blue	Open sunny areas	Vetches, clovers, alfalfa, other legumes	Nectar, puddling	South: Feb–Nov (3 +) North: May–Sep (2)	Larva
Western tailed blue	Open brushy areas	Vetches, milk vetches, and other legumes	Nectar, puddling	East: Apr–Jul (1) West: Mar–Apr (1 +)	Larva
Silvery blue	Open areas	Lupine and other legumes	Nectar, puddling	South: Mar–Apr (1) North: May–Jun (1)	Pupa

SNOUT AND HACKBERRY BUTTERFLIES

Hackberry Butterfly — *Asterocampa celtis*
Tawny Emperor — *Asterocampa clyton*

Snout Butterfly — *Libytheana bachmanii*

Snout and hackberry butterflies belong to different families, but they are grouped here because they share the same food plant — hackberry trees.

Snout butterflies belong to the snout family (Libytheidae), a small family with only two species in North America. They are the Cyranos of the butterfly world, named for their long mouthparts, which project forward like an extended beak. When perched with wings closed and head down, they resemble a leaf with its attaching stem. They may be seen in backyards.

The hackberry butterfly and tawny emperor are medium-sized butterflies that belong to the family of hackberry butterflies (Apaturidae). They are usually found near hackberry trees (*Celtis* spp.) but are hard to follow because they fly quickly and strongly. These two species are less common in backyards than snout butterflies and are more often found near natural vegetation.

Caterpillar Protection

Tawny emperors lay their eggs in large clusters of 50 to 500; they place the eggs on larger, older leaves for added concealment, even though younger leaves are better for the caterpillars to eat. Tawny emperors also stack some eggs on top of others. Eggs in the middle of clusters or in larger masses are more protected and less parasitized by wasps.

The sight and odor of frass (fecal droppings) make caterpillars more easily discovered by predators. A marvelous behavior that reduces predation on these caterpillars is site cleaning. Tawny emperor caterpillars bite the pellets of frass they produce and remove them from the leaves on which they are feeding.

This snout butterfly is beautifully camouflaged as a leaf on a twig.

Snout Butterfly

How to Attract

Adults: Snouts visit a wide range of flowers. Hackberry butterflies and tawny emperors are more attracted to sap and rotting fruit. You might try putting some fruit out specifically for them if they are in your area.

Larvae: These butterflies lay their eggs almost exclusively on hackberry trees. You can plant hackberries in your yard, or you may have some already lining your street if you live in the South.

Hackberry butterflies may visit flowers, but they are more commonly seen feeding on fruit or sap.

Hackberry Butterfly

This is a male tawny emperor; the female is paler overall.

Tawny Emperor

Streetlights and Housepainters

Snouts are not migratory on a regular basis but do occasionally move in vast numbers, especially in southwestern states. Once, in Arizona, streetlights were turned on in the middle of the day when a huge migration of snouts darkened the skies.

The year 1980 was a good year for hackberry butterflies and tawny emperors. In the deep South, the numbers of both species soared, as they do unpredictably in certain years. There were so many hackberry butterflies in one part of Louisiana that many stuck to the outside of a house

that was being painted, leading to litigation between homeowner and housepainter.

High-Protein Menu

Hackberry butterflies feed mostly on rotting fruit, carrion, and dung. As unappetizing as these foods may seem, they provide protein that is often lacking in nectar. When hackberry butterflies do visit flowers, as has been observed on snakewood flowers (*Colubrina* spp.) in Texas, they appear to be collecting protein from secretions within the flowers. Mostly females are found on these flowers, for they need extra protein to produce eggs.

Snout and Hackberry Butterflies

Snouts: 4–8 days? 2–3 weeks? 7–14 days? 4–12 days?
Hackberries: 3–9 days 4–6 weeks 7–10 days 6–14 days

Common Name	Habitat	Larval Food	Adult Food	Flight Period (Broods)	Winter Stage
Hackberry butterfly	Open woods	Hackberry	Sap, carrion, fruit, dung, nectar	South: Mar–Nov (2 +) North: Jun–Sep (2)	Larva
Tawny emperor	Forests near streams	Hackberry	Sap, carrion, fruit, dung, nectar	South: Mar–Nov (3) North: Jun–Aug (1)	Larva
Snout butterfly	Open brushy areas	Hackberry	Nectar, rotting fruit, puddling	South: All year (2–4) North: Mar–Nov (2)	Adult

LONGWINGS

Gulf Fritillary — *Agraulis vanillae*
Zebra — *Heliconius charitonius*

Gulf fritillaries and zebras are medium-sized members of a subfamily of tropical butterflies, known as longwings (Heliconiinae) because of their proportions. This subfamily belongs to the larger family of brush-footed butterflies (Nymphalidae), so named because their first pair of legs is small and covered with tiny hairs. Longwings cannot survive cold and so are restricted to the deep South in winter, but they may migrate up through the plains states during summer. All longwings choose passionflowers (family Passifloraceae) as food plants.

A Passionate Relationship

Passionflowers contain poisons — alkaloids and cyanogenic glycosides — that longwing caterpillars are able to ingest without harm, making them

This gulf fritillary with its wings closed reveals a stunning pattern underneath.

Gulf Fritillary

and the adult butterflies distasteful to predators such as birds and lizards. The adults' bright colors advertise this distastefulness to predators, who learn to leave these butterflies alone. Many other tropical butterflies mimic zebras and their relatives and thus gain protection from predators.

In a tropical forest, passionflowers are small, infrequent, and grow slowly. They also have several defenses against longwing caterpillars. First, they produce growths mimicking butterfly eggs, which may cause a female longwing to avoid the plant. Second, passionflowers attract ants to nectar produced on the leaves rather than in flowers, and the swarming ants attack eggs and caterpillars, as well as other insects found on the leaves. The nectar also attracts other enemies of caterpillars, including parasitic wasps.

Female longwings lay their eggs only on growing tips of the vines, where there is little nectar and consequently few ants. In addition, only one to a few eggs are laid on a single plant, since caterpillars can eat a lot and occasionally eat each other. Thus, to produce many young, a female zebra has to spend a lot of time finding food plants. To do so, she must live a long time, and she does — for up to five months.

Living for so long and continually producing eggs requires a steady source of protein in addition to sugar. Zebras and other longwings meet their

How to Attract

Adults: The zebra prefers moist tropical forests, while the gulf fritillary prefers open areas. Try planting lantana to attract gulf fritillaries.

Larvae: Their food plant, passionflowers, can be purchased in most southern nurseries and makes a nice garden plant as well.

A zebra stopping to feed on the nectar of butterfly weed. Its long wings make it easy to identify.

Zebra

protein needs by eating pollen. They gather pollen on their mouth parts and consume the nutrients released gradually through the chemical action of their saliva on the pollen. They are the only butterflies known to do this.

A female must feed on pollen for several days before she can even begin laying eggs. Thereafter, one large load of pollen gives her enough protein for the approximately five eggs she lays in a single day. Without pollen, females can live for only about one month.

When a Fritillary Is Not a Fritillary

The gulf fritillary is a longwing even though it is called a fritillary due to similar coloration. Although it originated in tropical forests, it has evolved in more open habitats and so is quite dif-

ferent from the zebra. Its wings are not as long; it flies longer distances and returns less to home ranges; it is not as bad tasting to birds; it does not live as long; and it feeds only on nectar. Its colors seem to camouflage it in its sunny environment, as is the case for the true fritillaries, distant relatives of the longwings.

Young Brides

Female zebra pupae release an odor that attracts males, who do not even wait for the females to emerge; they mate while the females are still in their pupal cases but fully developed. During mating the male transfers a chemical to the female which repels other males. This chemical "chastity belt" indicates to others that she has already mated and will not respond to courtship.

Longwings

Gulf fritillary:	○	4–8 days		2–3 weeks		5–10 days		2–4 weeks	
Zebra:		4–8 days		2–3 weeks		5–10 days		1–5 months	

Common Name	Habitat	Larval Food	Adult Food	Flight Period (Broods)	Winter Stage
Gulf fritillary	Open areas	Passionflowers	Nectar, some puddling	South: All year (4+) North: May–Sep (1)	Adult
Zebra	Forest edges	Passionflowers	Nectar, some puddling	South: All year (4+) North: May–Sep (1)	Adult

ANGLEWINGS AND TORTOISESHELLS

Milbert's Tortoiseshell — *Nymphalis (or Aglais) milberti*
Mourning Cloak — *Nymphalis antiopa*

Comma (Hop Merchant) — *Polygonia comma*
Question Mark — *Polygonia interrogationis*

Anglewings and tortoiseshells belong to a large subfamily of the brush-footed butterflies called varied brushfoots (Nymphalinae). Also in this subfamily are the butterflies in the next chapter — the ladies, the red admiral, and the buckeye. The varied brushfoots include many large and beautiful species. Most are distinctively colored on the upper surface of the wings, but when they land and fold their wings, they often mimic dead leaves or blend into the background. They are hard to follow because they fly so quickly and strongly in a somewhat jerky manner.

Note the shiny question mark design on the hind wing of this question mark butterfly.

On Anglewings and Tortoiseshells

Anglewings are named for the jagged edges to their wings; even their genus name, *Polygonia*, means "many angles." They are all orange-brown butterflies with dark markings on the upper wing surfaces and cryptic colors underneath. When disturbed, they perch head down on tree trunks and close their wings, exposing a camouflaged gray-to-brown surface with ragged edges that blends perfectly with tree bark. Sometimes they perch on branches and resemble dead leaves.

Anglewings include all butterflies whose names sound like punctuation marks. Question marks and commas are so named for the conspicuous, silvery, curved mark on the underside of their hind wings. Question mark butterflies, the largest of our anglewings, also have a silvery dot next to the commalike mark; they were known in the 1800s as violet tips for the violet sheen on the edges and undersides of their wings. Another name for the comma is hop merchant, because the

How to Attract

Adults: These butterflies prefer open woods. In spring you might try breaking a small branch of a birch or maple to attract them to the dripping sap. They are especially attracted to the freshly cut stumps of these trees because of the sap.

Larvae: Three of these species feed on nettles. This plant has stinging spines and should not be handled. However, false nettle (*Boehmeria* spp.) does not have stinging spines and is also accepted as a food plant. Elms and hackberries will also attract some of these species.

Other: Log piles, brush piles, or loose bark attached to trees may provide overwintering sites for adults.

You can compare this question mark with the similar comma below. Note the distinctive longer tails of the question mark.

Question Mark

larvae feed on cultivated hops and because the metallic spots on the pupae were used to forecast hop prices; silver spots meant prices low, gold spots meant prices high.

Like anglewings, tortoiseshells have jagged wing margins and are camouflaged underneath. However, they are more brightly and distinctly marked on the upper surfaces of their wings. The mourning cloak and Milbert's tortoiseshell are the two examples shown here.

Spring and Winter Behavior

You see these butterflies in forest openings or forest edges, but almost never on flowers. In spring you may see them feeding on tree sap, especially from trees with sugary sap, such as maples or birches. A broken branch where sap drips out or a recently cut stump is a good place to look for anglewings or tortoiseshells on a warm spring day. At other times of year they may feed on rotting fruit or carrion.

Anglewings overwinter as adults and may emerge to fly about on any warm winter day. People have unintentionally improved overwintering

The comma has the same general coloration as the question mark but has noticeably shorter tails.

Comma

The mourning cloak is distinctive with its dark wings and yellow edging.

Mourning Cloak

habitats for these butterflies by providing wood piles, houses, and outbuildings, all of which offer protected sites in which they can wait for warmer temperatures.

The Life of a Mourning Cloak

Mourning cloaks are among the more easily identified and widespread butterflies. They also hold the record for life span — some may live as long as 10 months as adults.

The adults overwinter in protected crevices such as under loose bark, in log piles, or in the nooks and crannies of buildings. When the temperature gets to about 60°F they may become active and fly about, even if it is still winter. This is why mourning cloaks are often the first butterflies seen in the spring, basking in the sun's rays with their wings outspread. At this season they always look worn because they have been alive since the past fall. They are frequently seen in spring feeding from tree sap or from early blooming shrubs such as willows, or gliding through the woods.

Males perch on shrubs or tree trunks and fly out after females during courting. Sometimes two

mourning cloaks may spiral up into the air together, but the function of these flights is not yet understood.

Females lay eggs in clusters on willows, elms, birches, and several other tree species. The caterpillars feed together, sometimes lined up side by side with their heads at the edge of the leaf. They are covered with spines and hairs that deter predators; such protection is needed because the caterpillars are conspicuous due to their number and the damage they create on their food plants. They go their separate ways just before pupating.

The adults from the first brood are flying about by early summer. It is believed that in many cases the adults go into a summer hibernation, called aestivation, and then emerge again in fall and feed before finding a protected place in which to spend the winter.

Defending Territories

Male commas and mourning cloaks are territorial; they choose certain sites that they defend against intruding males while waiting for females to fly by. Male commas defend and patrol their territories in much the same way as birds. They com-

This Milbert's tortoiseshell is basking on the trunk of a tree.

Milbert's Tortoiseshell

pete for the best territories, and, because the territories are small (20 square yards), they fly periodically from perch to perch while on the watch for intruders.

Male mourning cloaks defend large territories of more than 300 square yards. This increases the chances of a female's flying through but makes them harder to defend. More males fly through and must be chased, and more energy must be spent simply in surveying the entire territory. Consequently, a male mourning cloak moves frequently from perch to perch to see who may be in his territory, but he patrols only for short spells and through only a small portion of the territory at a time, apparently to conserve energy. Within their territories, these butterflies are aggressive; they have been reported to chase birds and everything else that flies near them.

Anglewings and Tortoiseshells

4–14 days   3–4 weeks   7–18 days   6–20 days

Common Name	Habitat	Larval Food	Adult Food	Flight Period (Broods)	Winter Stage
Milbert's tortoiseshell	Open areas near streams	Nettles	Nectar, some sap and fruit	South: Jun–Sep (2) North: Jun–Sep (1)	Adult
Mourning cloak	Open areas	Willows, aspens, elms, birches, hackberry	Sap, fruit, rarely nectar, puddling	South: Apr–Nov (1–2) North: Apr–Nov (1–2)	Adult
Comma	Forested areas	Hops, nettles, elms	Sap, carrion, fruit, dung	South: May–Oct (2) North: Jun–Oct (2)	Adult
Question mark	Open areas near forests	Elms, hackberry, hops, nettles	Sap, carrion, fruit, dung, puddling	South: Apr–Sep (2–4) North: May–Oct (2)	Adult

PAINTED LADIES, RED ADMIRAL, BUCKEYE

Buckeye — *Junonia coenia*
American Painted Lady — *Vanessa virginiensis*
Painted Lady — *Vanessa cardui*

Red Admiral — *Vanessa atalanta*
West Coast Lady — *Vanessa annabella* (or *V. carye*)

The ladies, the red admiral, and the buckeye belong to the large subfamily of butterflies known as varied brushfoots (Nymphalinae), along with the anglewings and tortoiseshells. This subfamily in turn belongs to the family of brush-footed butterflies (Nymphalidae).

The ladies and red admiral are all in the genus *Vanessa*. The buckeye is in the genus *Junonia* and shares some of the same behavior. All are medium-sized, generally dark butterflies with strong, fast, zigzagging flight that makes them hard to keep in sight, though buckeyes do not fly as strongly as the others. They all overwinter as adults.

A buckeye perched in a good position for basking, seeking sun on its upper surface. The large eyespots on fore and hind wings are the key to recognizing it.

Buckeye

Northward, Ho!

The painted lady, red admiral, and buckeye migrate from southern to northern areas each spring and summer. However, they do not make distinct southward migrations in fall after they have stopped breeding. Most die in the cold northern temperatures; numbers in the North are replenished the following year by new migrants.

Individual painted ladies can fly more than 600 miles and occasionally are seen far from land, such as out in the Atlantic Ocean. Painted ladies appear in huge numbers in some years, but infrequently or not at all in others. There is one report of 3 billion painted ladies sighted in a single northward migration in California. Large numbers of red admirals have also been seen migrating into Maine.

How to Attract

Adults: Painted ladies and buckeyes prefer open areas with low vegetation and a variety of flowers from which to sip nectar. Buckeyes also need bare earth, such as a dirt road or disturbed area, where males can perch while seeking mates. Red admirals need moist woods edges, where adults court and feed on sap.

Larvae: Try planting snapdragons for buckeyes and everlastings for American painted ladies. Wild plants to be encouraged include thistles for painted ladies, various mallows for West Coast ladies, and nettles for red admirals. However, nettles are invasive plants and have poisonous spines that should not be touched.

Other: Log piles, abandoned sheds, and loose bark on trees may provide shelter in warmer areas where adults survive through winter.

A painted lady can be distinguished from other ladies by the white crescent at the front edge of the forewing. Other ladies have orangish crescents.

Painted Lady

Territorial Defense

Male red admirals defend territories that tend to be elliptical and aligned with visually distinct features in the environment, such as a row of trees or a sidewalk. Within the territories, males choose brighter areas in which to perch and watch for intruders or possible mates. They fly out to investigate whatever comes by, whether it is another butterfly, a bird, or even a person; if you walk through his territory, a male red admiral may fly up to you briefly and then return to his perch.

Males chase birds or other species of butterflies off the territory and then return to their perches. When the territory-holder is chasing a male red admiral, the two spiral upward, enabling the original male to return to the middle of his territory more rapidly if a female or another male flies in.

Because males wander widely in search of sap, fruit, dung, or nectar each morning, they generally establish new territories each afternoon.

Sweet Treat

Different flowers produce nectar with different concentrations of sugars. Should a butterfly prefer a concentrated nectar or a dilute nectar? You might expect that the concentrated food would be chosen. It has been shown, though, that painted ladies can feed on dilute nectar more rapidly than on concentrated nectar, and as a result, they get a full meal, providing the maximum amount of energy, in less time.

Seeing Green

Butterflies are better than people in recognizing different shades of green, for their eyes have different color receptors than ours. This ability helps them pick out their food plants.

The ladies and red admiral have four different types of color receptors, each responding most to either red, green, blue, or ultraviolet light. Ultraviolet receptors enable butterflies to see outside the red-to-blue part of the spectrum, so they see patterns in flowers and other butterflies that we do not. In essence, they can see a wider range of colors.

This red admiral is perched on a tree, a site these butterflies often prefer. The red admiral is distinctive with orange-red bands crossing the dark wings.

Red Admiral

An American painted lady can be recognized by the two large eyespots on the undersides of the hind wings.

American Painted Lady

In addition to the four broad color receptors, these butterflies have other cells that are "turned on" by specific colors of light and whose response to different shades of green can be modified through learning. Butterflies cannot distinguish all shades of green, but they are remarkably well equipped to recognize different plants.

Buckeye Bonding

From morning to midafternoon, male buckeyes may be found perching on bare ground, such as a disturbed area, a dirt road, or a bare area of a field. In cool weather they may perch with wings open to bask, but when it is hotter they perch with wings closed.

If a male sees another male buckeye flying overhead, he flies up to investigate, pursues the male a short distance, and then returns to his perch on the ground.

If he discovers a female flying overhead he pursues her until she lands. He then hovers briefly above her before settling behind her and continuing to beat his wings more slowly. The female may fly off a short distance, in which case the male repeats his display. If the female is receptive, mating will eventually occur and may last for up to one-half hour.

The West Coast lady
is similar to American
painted lady on top,
but has small rather
than large eyespots
underneath.

West Coast Lady

Painted Ladies, Red Admiral, Buckeye

4–14 days	2–4 weeks	7–14 days	6–20 days

Common Name	Habitat	Larval Food	Adult Food	Flight Period (Broods)	Winter Stage
Buckeye	Low, weedy areas	Plantains, snapdragons	Nectar, puddling	South: All year (3+) North: Jun–Oct (1)	Adult
American painted lady	Moist open areas	Everlasting, pussytoes, and related composites	Nectar, puddling	South: All year (2+) North: Mar–Oct (1)	Adult
Painted lady	All open areas	Thistles, other composites, hollyhocks, borages	Nectar	South: All year (2+) North: Mar–Nov (1)	Adult
Red admiral	Moist woods edges	Nettles	Sap, fruit, dung, nectar	South: All year (2–4) North: Jun–Sep (1–2)	Adult
West Coast lady	Open sunny areas	Mallows, nettles	Nectar, dung	Most: Jun–Sep (2) Southwest: All year (3+)	Adult

FRITILLARIES

Meadow Fritillary — *Boloria (or Clossiana) bellona*
Great Spangled Fritillary — *Speyeria cybele*

Fritillaries are in the family of brush-footed butterflies (Nymphalidae). The name fritillary comes from the Latin word for "dice box," suggested by the checkered pattern of orange and black on the upper surface of this group's wings.

The largest fritillaries are called greater fritillaries or silver spots (genus *Speyeria*). The latter name is attributable to the beautiful large spots of silver on the underwing surfaces of most of these butterflies. Greater fritillaries use violets (*Viola* spp.) as food plants. They fly strongly and rapidly and are hard to follow in flight, but can be approached closely when they stop to drink nectar.

The lesser fritillaries, such as the meadow fritillary, are smaller members of this group and have varied patterns on the undersurface of their wings. They may choose other food plants in addition to violets, and fly more slowly and closer to the ground. Lesser fritillaries live mostly in the North.

What Species Is This?

In the West, species of fritillaries can be hard to tell apart, even for experts. At any single location, one fritillary species can be told from others by subtle differences in the colors and patterns of the underwings. But in another location, the same species can look different.

This occurs because populations of the same species have become isolated through climatic changes from glacial advances and retreats. Isolated populations sometimes remain very similar genetically but have evolved subtle differences in appearance.

Many fritillaries look so much alike, you may wonder how males and females find the right spe-

A great spangled fritillary perched at the tip of an old mullein stalk.

Great Spangled Fritillary

How to Attract

Adults: Fritillaries love to sip nectar at large composites like black-eyed Susans and daisies, but also visit many other flowers like clovers.

Larvae: To encourage violets to grow, provide them with a partially shaded environment.

Four meadow fritillaries getting nutrients from a carnivore scat.

Meadow Fritillary

cies for mating. The answer is: by smell. Females release odors from glands at the tips of their abdomens to attract the right males, while males release odors from their wings that stimulate females of their species. Smells are most likely sensed through the butterflies' antennae.

Locals and Wanderers

Some species of fritillaries have populations that are very narrowly distributed. Because these populations are isolated, when something happens to their environment there is a greater chance that they can become locally extinct. This has happened to the regal fritillary (*Speyeria idalia*), which is now absent from much of New England, where it used to be more common.

Other species of fritillaries wander widely to wherever they can find violets and nectar. A good example of this occurred in response to the 1980 eruption of the volcano Mount St. Helens in Washington. After the eruption, some fritillary populations were dramatically reduced or eliminated from the area, while others rapidly colonized the new open ash flows where violets were springing up.

Long Summer

Violets grow primarily in spring, and some fritillaries have timed their life cycle to fit this pattern. For example, great spangled fritillaries emerge from pupae and mate early in summer, but females delay laying eggs for 2 to 3 months, until late summer. The caterpillars hatch in fall, eat their eggshell, and immediately become inactive for the winter. The next spring, when violets are vigorously growing, the caterpillars resume feeding and complete their life cycle. Thus, great spangled fritillaries have only one brood per year.

Fritillaries

Meadow fritillary:	🥚 5–9 days	🐛 3–4 weeks	🦋 7 days	🦋 6–14 days
Great spangled fritillary:	10–15 days	Overwinters	14–24 days	2–10 weeks

Common Name	Habitat	Larval Food	Adult Food	Flight Period (Broods)	Winter Stage
Meadow fritillary	Open, moist areas	Violets	Nectar, dung	East: May–Sep (2–3) West: Jun–Jul (1)	Larva
Great spangled fritillary	Open areas	Violets	Nectar	South: Jun–Sep (1) North: Jun–Sep (1)	Larva

CRESCENTS AND CHECKERSPOTS

Baltimore — *Euphydryas phaeton*
Pearl Crescent (Pearly Crescentspot) — *Phyciodes tharos*

Crescents and checkerspots are small to medium-sized butterflies that form a subfamily (Melitaeinae) in the large family of brush-footed butterflies (Nymphalidae). All lay eggs in clusters (of up to 600) and the caterpillars feed communally. Adults are easy to follow because their flight is slow and usually just above the vegetation.

Crescents are the smaller of the two, typically orange with extensive dark-brown markings. Their name comes from a small, light crescent near the edge of their hind wings underneath. Their food plants are primarily in the daisy family (Asteraceae). Pearl crescents are among the most widespread North American butterflies, living in open areas wherever asters, their particular food plants, grow.

Checkerspots, including the Baltimore, are medium-sized butterflies, with a more distinctive spotting pattern than crescents. Their food plants are primarily in the figwort family (Scrophulariaceae). Baltimores are very local in occurrence due to the local distribution of their food plants — mainly turtlehead (*Chelone* spp.). Baltimores are named for the early American colonist George Calvert, the first Lord Baltimore, whose crest was orange and black. These colors are also the reason the northern oriole used to be called the Baltimore oriole.

Plant Poisons and Close Approach

Checkerspots lay their eggs on plants from several different families, but what the plants all have in common is the presence of toxins known as iridoid glycosides. Checkerspots accumulate plant poisons from their food plants. Predators quickly learn that checkerspot colors are associated with bad taste and avoid them.

Instead of closing their wings and being wary about predators, checkerspots spread their wings to advertise their distastefulness. Because of this, they are often easy to spot and can be approached closely.

How to Attract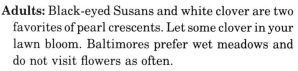

Adults: Black-eyed Susans and white clover are two favorites of pearl crescents. Let some clover in your lawn bloom. Baltimores prefer wet meadows and do not visit flowers as often.

Larvae: Grow asters in your garden to attract female pearl crescents. Although Baltimores prefer turtlehead as a host, an easier plant to provide is a common weed, the narrow-leaved plantain, which they might use.

The black background with white and orange dots along the margins of the wing can help you recognize the Baltimore.

Baltimore

This pearl crescent is perched in a typical pose — with its wings spread open.

Pearl Crescent

In Defense of Caterpillars

Checkerspot eggs, caterpillars, and pupae are all bad tasting to predators due to the plant poisons the caterpillars consume. Interestingly, the presence of these poisons actually stimulates the caterpillars to eat.

The caterpillars are also protected by their behavior. Once hatched, they crawl to the top of the food plant and spin a communal web around the leaves they will eat. They continue to extend the web to enclose new leaves. The web protects them, especially during the vulnerable times when they are shedding their skins.

Despite the webs, caterpillars are frequently exposed to predators and parasites, either when on the surface of the webs, where the caterpillars may bask, or just inside. When disturbed, they jerk their heads back and forth to deter wasps or knock them away. They can also regurgitate on a wasp, most likely with the plant poisons they have consumed; wasps spend considerable time cleaning themselves after encountering this defense. When faced with danger, caterpillars may also just crawl into the web or drop off the plant to escape.

Sun and Size

Size affects the activities of butterflies. Because female Baltimores are almost twice as large as males (and heavier because they carry eggs), they fly sluggishly. But their size also means they lose heat more slowly and can remain active longer away from direct sunlight than males. Males must bask more frequently just to maintain a warm body temperature. However, males warm up more quickly early in the day and are stronger fliers.

Crescents and Checkerspots

Baltimore:	○	14–20 days		Overwinters		14–18 days	6–10 days
Pearl crescent:		4–10 days		3 weeks		5–12 days	4–10 days

Common Name	Habitat	Larval Food	Adult Food	Flight Period (Broods)	Winter Stage
Baltimore	Wet meadows	Turtlehead, plantains	Nectar	South: May–Jul (1) North: May–Jul (1)	Larva
Pearl crescent	Open areas	Asters	Nectar, puddling	South: All year (5–6) North: May–Oct (1–2)	Larva

ADMIRALS

Sister — *Adelpha bredowii*
Lorquin's Admiral — *Limenitis (or Basilarchia) lorquini*
Red-Spotted Purple — *Limenitis (or Basilarchia) arthemis astyanax*
White Admiral (Banded Purple) — *Limenitis (or Basilarchia) arthemis arthemis*
Viceroy — *Limenitis (or Basilarchia) archippus*
Western Admiral (Weidemeyer's Admiral) — *Limenitis (or Basilarchia) weidemeyerii*

These butterflies are in the subfamily of admirals and sisters (Limenitidinae), which in turn is in the large family of brush-footed butterflies (Nymphalidae). Long ago in England, a white-banded butterfly was known as a white "admirable" because of its beauty. Over time this name was modified and given to its North American relatives, the butterflies shown here.

Admirals and sisters are a closely related group of butterflies, and most have broad white stripes across both forewings and hind wings. The white bands on the dark background are in part disruptive coloration, breaking up the recognizable form of the butterfly to potential predators. The white bands, as well as the orange wing tips of some admirals, may also draw a predator's at-

tention away from the vulnerable body. The caterpillars and even the pupae mimic bird droppings.

Admirals cruise through the air with a characteristic sailing flight and can move away powerfully when disturbed. Although it has a similar name, the red admiral is not closely related to this group.

Several Mimics

Admirals are tasty to predators and must avoid being too catchable or conspicuous. Some species have lost the bold white-stripe pattern and have evolved to look like unpalatable butterflies, and are thus avoided by avian predators such as jays.

A good example is the red-spotted purple, which mimics the pipevine swallowtail, a species that is black with a blue-green sheen and has noxious chemicals in its body from its food plant, pipevine. (See Swallowtails, page 44.) The mimicry is not perfect, but good enough to slow a predator down and give the butterfly a chance to escape.

Another butterfly in this group that mimics a bad-tasting species is the viceroy. Through most of their range, viceroys mimic monarchs, with black wing veins on an orange background. Vice-

This red-spotted purple is a relative of the white admiral and a mimic of the pipevine swallowtail.

Red-Spotted Purple

How to Attract

Adults: The admirals eat a wide variety of foods, including nectar, sap, and nutrients from carrion, dung, and puddles. Providing any or some of these may attract adults for feeding.

Larvae: Many of the food plants for this group are in the willow family (Salicaceae), including aspens, willows, cottonwoods, and poplars. Encouraging any of these on your property may attract egg-laying females.

The viceroy is a good mimic of the monarch and queen except for the extra black line across its hind wings.

Viceroy

roys are such excellent mimics of monarchs that it is hard for beginning butterfly-watchers to distinguish between the two.

In Florida, queens are more common than monarchs, so Florida viceroys are darker brown to better resemble the bad-tasting queens. There is evidence, too, that viceroys are somewhat bad tasting on their own, but they clearly gain an advantage by mimicking monarchs and queens.

Lorquin's admirals may even be mimics of the similar sisters. Sisters feed on oaks and may be distasteful to birds, but this needs further study.

One Species, Two Forms

To us, white admirals and red-spotted purples look like very different butterflies. But despite the differences in appearance, they are considered to be members of the same species because they readily interbreed. Hybrids have some characteristics of both white admirals and red-spotted purples and occur from southern Maine and Massachusetts westward through New York, Pennsylvania, lower Michigan, and Wisconsin to Minnesota and Iowa. White admirals are common north of this zone, red-spotted purples to the south.

In the hybrid zone, if white admirals prefer to mate with white admirals and red-spotted purples

with red-spotted purples, then these two groups may evolve to become distinct species sometime in the future.

Why does this one species have two different forms, one in the South that looks like the pipe-

This white admiral shows how the white bands of admirals break up their overall shape and make them less recognizable to predators.

White Admiral

The sister is similar to Lorquin's admiral but has narrower white bands, and black surrounding its orange wing tips.

Sister

This western admiral has its wings closed, showing the white bands underneath as well.

Western Admiral

vine swallowtail and one in the North that looks like a normal admiral? Having white bands is the more primitive trait, so white admirals came first. The more southern members of this species overlapped the range of the pipevine swallowtail and gained some advantage by looking like it. The northern members did not and so remained unchanged.

Taking On Gulls

Western admirals defend open sites near waterways, from which they can watch any butterfly that flies through. If it is a male, they chase it; if it is a female, they court it. They are fearless when defending their sites, as is shown by the reported instance in British Columbia of a western admiral repeatedly chasing a glaucous-winged gull until it left the butterfly's territory.

Finding Butterflies in Winter

All species in this subfamily overwinter as small caterpillars temporarily stopped in the middle of their larval development. In fall, after eating away the tip of a leaf on either side of the midvein, they curl the base of the leaf into a little tube and secure it with silk. Before crawling inside for the

The Lorquin's admiral has wide white bands and orange extending to the edge of its wing tips.

Lorquin's Admiral

winter, they crawl to the base of the leaf and tie it firmly to the twig with a reinforcement of silk.

This tiny winter home is called a hibernaculum and, with a little diligence during a winter walk, you can find them attached to the food plants. Look for a small bit of leaf still attached to the twigs when most others have fallen off. Then check to see if it is tied on with silk. If so, then you have found a butterfly in winter.

In spring, the little caterpillars emerge from their leafy tubes. They resume eating and continue their development.

Admirals

○ 4–9 days   3–4 weeks   7–14 days   6–14 days?

Common Name	Habitat	Larval Food	Adult Food	Flight Period (Broods)	Winter Stage
Sister	Oak woods, canyons	Oaks	Nectar, fruit, puddling	South: Apr–Oct (2+) North: Jun–Aug (1)	Larva
Lorquin's admiral	Moist canyons	Willows, aspens, cottonwoods, chokecherry	Nectar, puddling	South: Apr–Oct (1–2) North: Jun–Aug (1)	Larva
Red-spotted purple	Moist forests, willows	Wild cherry, aspens, poplars	Nectar, carrion, fruit, dung, sap	South: Mar–Nov (2–3) North: May–Nov (2)	Larva
White admiral	Birch, aspen forests	Birches, aspens	Nectar, carrion, fruit, dung, sap	South: May–Sep (2) North: Jun–Aug (1)	Larva
Viceroy	Moist shrubby areas	Willows, aspens, cottonwoods, some fruit trees	Nectar, sap, dung, puddling	South: Apr–Dec (3) North: Jun–Sep (2)	Larva
Western admiral	Moist canyons	Willows, aspens, cottonwoods	Nectar, carrion, sap, puddling	South: May–Aug (2) North: Jun–Jul (1)	Larva

SATYRS

Common Wood Nymph — *Cercyonis pegala*
Ringlet — *Coenonympha tullia*
Little Wood Satyr — *Megisto cymela*
Northern Eyed Brown — *Satyrodes eurydice*

Satyrs are medium-sized, brownish butterflies, often with eyespots underneath. They belong to the family of satyrs (Satyridae), so called because of their dancing flight through the woodlands.

Once disturbed, satyrs can be hard to follow, for after flying rapidly away from a disturbance, they often drop into the grass or land quickly against a shaded tree trunk or on a leaf. Remaining still, with their wings held together and tilted to avoid casting a shadow, they are well hidden. Their home is frequently a partially shaded woods,

The ringlet is variable but is usually orange-brown to tan, small, and plain. It sometimes has eyespots.

Ringlet

and with weak flight ability, they seldom wander far from it. All choose grasses and sedges for food plants.

We have chosen the northern eyed brown as a representative of several common but regionally distributed species that look similar, including all eyed browns (*Satyrodes* spp.) and pearly eyes (*Enodia* spp.). The other three are common species in wide areas.

Daily Life

Ringlets are good examples of how the activity of butterflies is affected by temperature. At 60°F, these butterflies spend most of the day perched on vegetation warming up in the sun. But when the air is warmer, above 75°F, they spend most of their time flying. This flight time is spent primarily searching for mates, with only a little time spent feeding.

Temperature, therefore, affects their mating strategy. When the air is warm, male butterflies search actively for mates by patrolling back and forth over grassy areas; but when the air is cool, they must sit on perches at the edge of woods and wait for a potential mate to fly by. From these

How to Attract

Adults: Open woods and tall grasses are habitats favored by satyrs, where they feed on tree sap oozing from wounds in bark or branches. Ringlets are unusual among satyrs in that they frequently feed on nectar from a variety of flowers.

Larvae: To attract egg-laying satyrs, try to let some part of your property grow tall with grasses. Just stop mowing a corner of your lawn and leave it for the satyrs.

The little wood satyr has eyespots on the upper surface as well as underneath, shown here.

Little Wood Satyr

perches, they fly out to investigate females or any other thing that comes their way, even people. While walking down a tree-lined path into a small clearing, you may suddenly be greeted and looked over by a curious satyr.

Spotting Predators

One thing you will notice about satyrs is that they look different from most other butterflies. Most are brown with striking eyespots on their wings. Why have they evolved this color pattern?

The drab colors of satyrs help them blend in with their background. This is their first line of defense, and it may be connected to having grasses as their food plants. Grasses do not contain the plant poisons common in other plants, and consequently the butterflies are tasty to bird predators. Other butterflies are often colorful because they are actually advertising their distastefulness. Satyrs keep quiet about being tasty.

When satyrs happen to be discovered by a predator, their eyespots become useful. Birds and lizards that attack satyrs leave beak and mouth marks along the margins of the wings, near the eyespots. This is because small eyespots, like those of the eyed brown, tend to attract predators, de-

flecting their attention from the more important, vulnerable body and leading them toward the wings.

Larger, pupiled eyespots, such as those of common wood nymphs, serve a different function. The butterfly suddenly opens its wings and flashes the eyespots in front of the predator. Because they look like the eyes of a larger animal, they startle the predator and give the butterflies a chance to escape.

Launching Eggs

Most female butterflies search carefully for plant locations on which to place their eggs. Satyrs may be careful as well, but it does not always seem that way. They all choose grasses and sedges as food plants, some using only one species and others using several. Although females sometimes place their eggs carefully on the leaves of their grass food, at other times they scatter their eggs from the air into vegetation in habitats with the right plants. Somehow, after hatching, the larvae then locate and crawl to plants they can eat. Such behavior may seem strange to us, but it works for them.

In the northern eyed brown, look for the three to four eyespots at the margins of both surfaces of forewings and hind wings.

Northern Eyed Brown

One Among Many

Ringlets are one of the smaller types of satyrs. Some lepidopterists (people who study butterflies and moths) say that there are many species of ringlets in North America. Others believe that they are all members of a Eurasian species called the large heath (*Coenonympha tullia*) and should be considered one species. We have followed this latter classification. Nonetheless, there are distinct forms of this species that you will see in various regions of the continent. Some of the more common are the California ringlet in the West, the ochraceous ringlet in the Rocky Mountains and the Southwest, and the inornate ringlet in north-central and northeast regions.

Range Expansion

Until recently, ringlets in the East were found only from the Canadian maritime provinces westward into Quebec and Ontario. In recent decades, they have expanded their range south. They moved down to the St. Lawrence River by the 1950s, to the upper fringe of the northern United States by the 1960s, and down the Lake Champlain–Hudson River and Connecticut River valleys by the 1970s. Today ringlets are found in much of New England and New York.

Accompanying this expansion in range is a shift from having only one generation per year to completing two generations per year. The longer growing season of more southerly areas is what allows this added generation to be squeezed in. But this change has coincided with more fundamental biological change. Genetic studies confirm this: southern ringlets are different from northern ringlets.

A possible cause for these changes may have been a warm period in the mid-1900s that allowed two-generation butterflies to develop in southern Ontario. After genetic changes took place in the butterflies, range expansion then followed.

In common wood nymphs, notice the lighter, yellowish area that surrounds the two dots on the forewings. These eyespots vary in brightness and size among individuals.

Common Wood Nymph

Satyrs

	6–20 days		3–4 weeks		10–16 days		6–14 days?

Common Name	Habitat	Larval Food	Adult Food	Flight Period (Broods)	Winter Stage
Common wood nymph	Open grassy areas, woods edges	Grasses	Plant juices, some nectar	South: Jun–Sep (1) North: Jul–Sep (1)	Larva
Ringlet	Open grassy areas	Grasses	Nectar	South: Jun–Sep (2) North: Jun–Jul (1)	Larva
Little wood satyr	Grassy woodlands	Grasses	Sap, rarely nectar	South: Apr–Sep (2–3) North: Jun–Jul (1)	Larva
Northern eyed brown	Marshes, wet meadows	Sedges	Sap, rarely nectar	South: Jun–Sep (1 +) North: Jun–Sep (1 +)	Larva

MILKWEED BUTTERFLIES

Monarch — *Danaus plexippus*
Queen — *Danaus gilippus*

The monarch and the queen belong to the family of milkweed butterflies (Danaidae), which consists primarily of large tropical butterflies. North American species of milkweed butterflies for the most part use milkweeds as their food plants, incorporating toxic substances into their bodies and becoming distasteful to predators.

A monarch feeding on goldenrod in late summer.

Monarch

The monarch and the queen are strong fliers, often alternating a few strong flaps with a long glide. They are easy to watch and can be approached quite closely, although when wanting to escape, they can fly extremely fast.

Spectacular Migration

Monarch butterflies cannot withstand freezing temperatures, so they migrate south for the winter. Monarchs in different regions of the continent have different migration behavior.

Those in eastern and central North America start south when late summer temperatures drop to 60°F. By utilizing soaring flight, which saves energy, they can fly several thousand miles sustained by the fat reserves stored in their bodies. They also feed some while flying south.

While moving south, they may roost in trees containing thousands of other monarchs. This may help them preserve warmth during cool nights. Some roosting trees are used year after

How to Attract

Adults: Monarchs and queens are generally attracted to taller flowers when looking for nectar, and they often come to gardens where there is a mass of bloom. They will also love a field or small area full of wildflowers such as asters, goldenrod, and thistle.

Larvae: You need milkweeds to attract the egg-laying females of these species. Common milkweed is not appropriate for a garden since it spreads by thick rhizomes, but if it is growing in a wild area, encourage it by keeping competing vegetation low. For the garden, an appropriate species is butterfly weed.

A close-up of just a few monarchs at their winter roost
in Mexico, where millions gather together.

A queen butterfly perched to catch the sun's warming rays.

Queen

year, leading to the suggestion that the butterflies may mark them with a scent, but this has not been proven.

Some of these monarchs winter on the Gulf Coast from Florida to southern Texas. Most monarchs from central and eastern North America migrate to specific areas in the mountains of northern Mexico, where they overwinter in huge aggregations. One site hosts about 13 million monarchs in an area of 3 to 4 acres.

The butterflies congregate in the central portion of tall trees, possibly to avoid cool winds above and occasional frost near the ground. During the day, they bask in the sun and may go to streams to drink. It is believed that they have enough fat stored in their bodies to last them through the winter without feeding, as long as they stay fairly inactive.

West Coast monarchs migrate in fall from northern regions to southern California and a few to Arizona. In warmer areas, they are free flying and do not join roosts. In cooler areas, they may form temporary roosts containing tens of thousands of butterflies.

Most monarchs mate while on the wintering grounds, just before migrating north in spring. It is mostly fertilized females that migrate north. Only about 1 percent of these travel all the way to northern states, laying eggs as they go. Following them is an influx of males and females matured from the first eggs laid on plants in southern states.

Adult monarchs that migrate to Mexico or overwinter in the South may live up to six months, but those that are actively reproducing in summer live only 60 to 70 days.

The Advantage of Bad Taste

Milkweeds contain toxins called cardiac glycosides. Monarch and queen caterpillars accumulate these toxins while feeding and become distasteful to predators such as birds and reptiles. The toxins remain even in the body of the adult butterfly, and in the monarch are concentrated in the wings and the abdomen.

Predators that eat one milkweed butterfly, or take a bite out of a wing, may begin to vomit and, thereafter, never try to eat one again. The bright orange and black of milkweed butterflies is believed to be a warning coloration — colors a predator will remember to avoid after trying once.

A recent study found that the level of toxins among milkweed plant species varies, and that some northern species contain practically none. Therefore, monarchs that feed on them are actually not distasteful, but they still gain some protection from predators by looking like other monarchs that are distasteful, a phenomenon called automimicry.

A typical view of monarchs during the day at their wintering areas in the mountains of Mexico.

Mating Behavior

Mating of monarchs and queens occurs mostly in midafternoon. In monarchs the male patrols over an area where milkweed grows. When he spots a female, he flies after her and dives at her, directing her flight down to the vegetation. He may even hold onto her body with his legs and then glide down with her. Once she is landed, he may again fly over her, and then alight alongside and join his abdomen to hers in copulation.

Following this, the two may fly up to 75 feet high and over 300 yards away, the male carrying the female suspended from his abdomen. This flight usually ends high up in trees, where the two remain joined for as much as an hour.

In the queen butterfly, courtship is similar except that at the start the male does not grab the female but hovers above her, releasing a scent that may make her receptive to mating.

Hair Pencils and Androconia

Male milkweed butterflies have small pouches on their hind wings that contain scent scales called androconia and small brushlike structures that can be extended from the tip of their abdomen called hair pencils. Both structures contain pheromones (male scent) used during courtship. The androconial pouches are visible as small swellings on the black veins of the hind wings, and they enable you to recognize males.

Hair pencils are extruded under pressure. They give off a dusting of pheromone onto the female when the male hovers over her in courtship. This is especially important in the queen. In the monarch the hair pencils seem to play a lesser role.

Milkweed Butterflies

4–6 days   2–3 weeks   5–15 days   1–3 months

Common Name	Habitat	Larval Food	Adult Food	Flight Period (Broods)	Winter Stage
Monarch	Open fields, roadsides	Milkweeds	Nectar	South: All year (4–6) North: Jun–Oct (1–4)	Adult
Queen	Open fields, roadsides	Primarily milkweeds	Nectar	South: All year (4+) North: Aug–Sep (1)	Adult

SKIPPERS

Silver-Spotted Skipper — *Epargyreus clarus*
Fiery Skipper — *Hylephila phyleus*
European Skipper — *Thymelicus lineola*
Long-Tailed Skipper — *Urbanus proteus*

Skippers are in the family of skippers (Hesperiidae), which contains many species of small orange to brown butterflies that are often hard to distinguish from one another. One trait that makes skippers distinctive is their rapidly darting flight — they "skip" about over the vegetation, seemingly with self-confidence and independence.

There are numerous superfamilies in the order Lepidoptera — one we know as butterflies, one as skippers, and the others as many different kinds of moths. In some ways skippers appear to be intermediate between butterflies and moths. Like butterflies, they fly during the day; but like moths, they have relatively heavy bodies and dull colors. There are some minor anatomical differences among the three groups: for example, moths have feathery or filamentous antennae; butterflies have antennae with rounded knobs; and skippers have knobbed antennae with little points or hooks at the tips of the knobs. While not true butterflies, skippers are related to them and are usually considered a type of butterfly.

Spotting Mates

Why should a butterfly like the silver-spotted skipper have such conspicuous silver marks on its wings? The marks are useful for recognizing other individuals of the same species, especially when males dart out from their perches to investigate other butterflies passing by.

Silver-spotted skippers occur widely, especially in moist areas where their food tree, black locust, is found. Sunlight streaming through the trees produces only spotty illumination, and conspicuous markings are necessary for identifying poten-

The long-tailed skipper is easy to recognize, because of its long tails.

Long-Tailed Skipper

How to Attract

Adults: The silver-spotted skipper and long-tailed skipper prefer brushy areas, while the smaller fiery and European skippers are happy in fields, lawns, and other grassy areas. All species feed on nectar from many different flowers.

Larvae: European skipper larvae are fond of timothy, a common grass of fields, and fiery skipper larvae will feed on a variety of common grasses, including, of all things, crabgrass — which makes them welcome in many yards.

The fiery skipper is a common visitor to backyard gardens.

Fiery Skipper

tial mates. White and silver marks seem to be typical of skipper species that fly in and out of shade or near dusk.

Perching

Most male skippers use a perch when trying to find females. A male perches on an open twig or grass blade that provides a good view, from which he can fly out to investigate any insect that goes through his territory. Males compete among themselves for the best sites, and they defend their sites from other males. When another male invades an occupied territory, the resident male flies out, and the two engage in a fast and aerobatic chase. Often another male sees the chase and joins in, and frequently the chase spirals upward. Silver-spotted skippers choose high perches in their lush habitats, and any person who walks near them is apt to be buzzed by a little butterfly. Fiery skippers, which live in low vegetation, choose perches much closer to the ground.

Sexing by Flight

Rather than perching, male European skippers spend more than half their time flying in a zigzag manner, patrolling for females. Having proportionally more wing area for their size, males have slower wingbeats and can fly in cooler conditions. They also fly closer to the ground, where they have a greater chance at finding unmated females.

Females spend less than 15 percent of their time in flight and fly more in a straight direction. These sexual differences in flight behavior are likely characteristics of any butterfly species in which the males are patrollers.

Lying in Wait

Visiting flowers for nectar is not always safe. Crab spiders lie concealed among the petals of flowers, blending in with the color of the petals, waiting for insects to come for nectar. After an insect lands, the spider can catch and eat it. Smaller

This European skipper is feeding on the nectar from red clover.

European Skipper

insects, including skippers, are typical prey.

Another hazard is being unable to escape from the flower itself. Lady's-slipper orchids are adapted to pollination by bees; when bees enter the opening to the floral chamber and become entrapped, they are strong enough to escape, transferring pollen in the process. But other insects are not able to escape. Up to 24 European skippers, along with other insects, have been found dead in a single lady's-slipper orchid.

Native North American skippers are not entrapped in these flowers, but the European skipper did not evolve in the presence of lady's-slippers and may have come to this continent with feeding behaviors that do not work with some native North American flowers.

Home on the Range

The European Skipper was introduced to North America sometime before 1910, when it was first reported in Ontario. Since then, its range has expanded rapidly, reaching Iowa by 1975, for example. It is now found in most of the Northeast, and has been reported in British Columbia as well, due to a recent separate introduction.

In agricultural areas, it can be the most abundant butterfly, occasionally becoming a pest. Because this butterfly lays its eggs on grasses in hayfields, transport of hay is a likely factor in its spread. An average of 5,000 live skipper eggs have been found per hay bale from fields with high populations. How far can the European skipper go? No one knows, but its range is still expanding.

A silver-spotted skipper feeding from a black-eyed
Susan that is just opening.

Silver-Spotted Skipper

Skippers

○ 4–7 days	🐛 3–5 weeks	🛏 12–14 days	🦋 10–20 days

Common Name	Habitat	Larval Food	Adult Food	Flight Period (Broods)	Winter Stage
Silver-spotted skipper	Forest edges	Black locust, woody legumes	Nectar, some puddling	South: Feb–Dec (3) North: May–Sep (1)	Larva or pupa
Fiery skipper	Open sunny areas	Grasses, including crabgrass	Nectar	South: All year (3–5) North: Apr–Nov (1)	Unknown
European skipper	Grassy fields	Grasses, especially timothy	Nectar	South: Jun–Aug (1) North: Jun–Aug (1)	Egg
Long-tailed skipper	Open areas	Beans and other climbing legumes	Nectar	South: All year (3) North: Jun–Aug (1)	Adult

RESOURCES

Butterfly Societies

Entomological Society of America, 9301 Annapolis Road, Lanham, MD 20706. A scientific society devoted to the study of all insects, including butterflies.

The Lepidopterists' Society, 257 Common Street, Dedham, MA 02026-4020. A society open to all interested in butterflies and moths. Publishes a scientific journal and newsletter.

Sonoran Arthropod Studies, Inc., P.O. Box 5624, Tucson, AZ 85703. An environmental education organization devoted to the enjoyment and study of butterflies and other arthropods.

The Xerces Society, 10 SW Ash Street, Portland, OR 97204. An international nonprofit organization dedicated to the global protection of habitats for butterflies and other invertebrates.

Young Entomologists' Society, 1915 Peggy Place, Lansing, MI 48910. A nonprofit society serving youth and amateur insect enthusiasts.

Butterfly Books

Brewer, Jo, and Dave Winter. 1986. *Butterflies and Moths*. New York: Prentice-Hall Press.

Feltwell, John. 1986. *The Natural History of Butterflies*. New York: Facts on File.

Mitchell, R. T., and H. S. Zim. 1964. *Butterflies and Moths*. New York: Golden Press.

Opler, Paul A., and George O. Krizek. 1984. *Butterflies East of the Great Plains*. Baltimore: Johns Hopkins University Press. A comprehensive account.

Pyle, Robert Michael. 1981. *The Audubon Society Field Guide to North American Butterflies*. New York: Alfred A. Knopf.

———. 1984. *The Audubon Society Handbook for Butterfly Watchers*. New York: Charles Scribner's Sons.

Scott, James A. 1986. *The Butterflies of North America*. Stanford, CA: Stanford University Press. A comprehensive account.

Tekulsky, Mathew. 1985. *The Butterfly Garden*. Boston: The Harvard Common Press.

Walton, Richard. 1990. *Familiar Butterflies*. New York: Alfred A. Knopf.

The Xerces Society / Smithsonian Institution. 1990. *Butterfly Gardening*. San Francisco: Sierra Club Books.

Butterfly Houses

These are places that have large conservatories filled with butterflies and plants. Being in any one of them is a very special and exciting experience. Call them to find out more.

Butterfly Exhibit. Marine World Africa–USA, Marine World Parkway, Vallejo, CA 94589. 707-643-6722.

Butterfly World. Port Alberni Highway, Coombs, British Columbia V0R 1M0. 604-248-7026.

Butterfly World. Tradewinds Park South, 3600 West Sample Road, Coconut Creek, FL 33073. 305-977-4400.

Day Butterfly Center. Callaway Gardens, Pine Mountain, GA 31822. 404-663-2281.

Insect World. Cincinnati Zoo and Botanical Garden, 3400 Vine Street, Cincinnati, OH 45220. 513-281-4701.

Papillon Park. 120 Tyngsboro Road, Westford, MA 01886. 508-392-0955.

Butterfly Feeders, Etc.

The Brown Company. 140 Dean Knauss Drive, Narragansett, RI 02882. 800-556-7670. Makes butterfly feeders and butterfly hibernation houses.